the prayers of
Catherine
of Siena

the
prayers of

atherine
of Siena

edited by
Suzanne Noffke, O.P.

paulist press *new york/ramsey*

Library of Congress
Catalog Card Number: 82-60746

ISBN: 0-8091-2508-0

Published by Paulist Press
545 Island Road, Ramsey, N.J. 07446

Printed and bound in the
United States of America

CONTENTS

Contents

INTRODUCTION

Catherine of Siena (1347–1380) was a woman whose living consistently grew out of her encounter with God, from the visionary experience that made her decide, in her childish way when she was only about six years old, to live for God alone, to the final mature offering of her life for the reform and unity of the Church at the age of thirty-three. Catherine's life is, in fact, defined by her prayer.

We learn some of the external details of this prayer from those who knew her and later wrote of what they had seen and heard: Raymond of Capua in bis *Legenda Major*,[1] Tommaso di Antonio da Siena in both expanded and abridged versions of Raymond's work,[2] and other disciples of hers in their letters[3] and in their testimony for the process of her canonization.[4] They tell us, for example, that Catherine's favorite times for prolonged prayer were after the morning's liturgy and in the early evening as well as during the long night hours when she scarcely slept; that she would frequently interrupt her business or conversations to "consult," as it were, with God; that she would easily be transported in her prayer into an ecstatic trance, losing use of all her senses except speech, and that often in such a trance she would pray aloud; that when she was not in a complete trance her prayer was physically very expressive: walking, kneeling, or prostrate on the floor, extending her arms or clasping her hands to her heart or striking her breast in contrition, gazing upward or closing her eyes. And we are told that when she prayed alone, especially in the garden, she liked to sing.

But far more significant than any of these external circumstances are the traits we can deduce from Catherine's own writings and those of her prayers which have actually been preserved for us. From these it is clear that Catherine, while very concerned about prayer, was very little concerned about "methods" of prayer. Her own prayer took many forms, and she was delighted to see many different ways of prayer in others. Repetitious as she could be in her writings and conversation, she had little personal patience with repetitive forms of prayer for herself once she had grown up; yet she would advise such prayer for those to whom it might be of value. The principles she emphasized in her teaching found constant expression in her own prayer: knowledge of God as loving redeemer and of herself as loved sinner, the centrality of truth and love, the primacy of desire, the call to enter fully into redemption by becoming herself redemptive. There is, interestingly, no evidence in her recorded prayers of anything resembling a "dark night" or "crisis of faith," though she does speak perceptively of such phenomena in her *Dialogue,*[5] probably from experiences during her three years of solitude before her active ministry began.

One factor that is very obvious—especially in the prayers in the present collection, since most of them were prayed immediately after the morning's liturgy—is the impact that daily liturgy and its biblical readings had on Catherine's thought and prayer. There was considerable variation in lectionaries from place to place in the fourteenth century, and therefore a really adequate commentary on this aspect of Catherine's prayer will have to await a study of the lectionaries in use at that time in the churches Catherine frequented for Mass. One cannot but be struck, however, in the instances where we do know the day's readings for certain, with the depth at which she appropriated these readings and integrated the whole complex of her own spiritual vision with them.

As deeply as Catherine plunged into meditation on the mysteries of faith, just so intimately did she keep touch with her day to day concerns. Almost invariably we find her prayer returning to the specific needs of the Church and of those she has "been given to love with a special love." And she holds these before God with a frankness and warmth that indicate well the nature of her relations with these persons and institutions in her actual converse with them.

THE PRAYERS AS A COLLECTION

A good number of Catherine's spoken prayers, though surely not nearly all of them, have been preserved for us by certain of her disciples who acted as her secretaries—some within the context of dictated letters (for she would burst into prayer while dictating as readily as she would during a conversation); some within her book, the *Dialogue;* some, whether from memory or from actual notes, as part of the narratives of her life; and some finally which were taken down, with or without her knowledge, as she prayed in ecstasy, and which eventually became part of a specific collection. It is the last group that forms the present volume.[6] These twenty-six prayers are all from the last four years of Catherine's life, most of them from her final seventeen months. They therefore, along with her letters of the same period, express Catherine's spirituality at its most mature level.

We are very seldom told in specific instances who recorded these prayers. Both Raymond of Capua and Tommaso Petra (at that time a papal notary in Avignon) seem to be given credit for the first two, while Raymond was also among those who might have witnessed the third, but none of the rest. Bartolomeo Dominici, Catherine's long-time close friend and her second confessor, tells us that he took down some of the prayers, and that just as many were taken down by others. Surely one of these others was Barduccio Canigiani, another close friend and one of her most constant secretaries, who was with her during her entire stay in Rome (Bartolomeo was absent at least during the early months of 1380 if not longer). Of her other chief secretaries, Neri di Landoccio Pagliaresi was also with her much of the time in Rome, and Stefano Maconi only at the very end. Stefano, however, as well as Neri, had been with her at Avignon, Genoa, Siena, and Rocca d'Orcia. Tommaso Caffarini's presence is a bit more difficult to determine. We know that he was among her earliest disciples, but though he wrote so much about her after her death we do not know whether he ever served as secretary to her, nor whether he might have actually recorded any of these prayers.

Unlike the manuscript tradition for Catherine's *Dialogue* and *Letters,* where the Italian text is clearly primary and very close if not identical to the original, these prayers come to us in parallel (though not always fully matching!) Italian and Latin versions (see Table I). The introductory rubric shared, with very minor variations, by three of the earliest extant manuscripts containing twenty-two of the prayers in Latin (R, S1, N) states that "they were taken down in Latin by one or several of her disciples, word by word, as this holy maiden offered them in her own dialect." Were none of them, then, actually recorded in Catherine's language? From the linguistic evidence of the text this is hard to believe, for in most cases the Italian seems the more original of the two versions. It may be true that one or the other of her secretaries did translate simultaneously into Latin as he listened and wrote, given the common prejudice of the time which assumed that no one who was educated enough to read at all would read anything but Latin. Yet there is also the established fact that these same secretaries had, less than a year before, taken down Catherine's dictation for the *Dialogue,* and translated that work into Latin only after her death. It might be argued that in the case of the *Dialogue* Catherine was exercising a proprietorship over the work that she apparently had no interest in where her prayers were concerned. Perhaps, then, some of the prayers were recorded in a simultaneous Latin translation and then later retranslated into Italian, while others were recorded in Italian to be translated later into Latin. For seven prayers, in fact, there is no extant manuscript version in Italian, while for every Italian manuscript version there is a Latin parallel.

The clue to the puzzle may well lie in the earliest known collection of the prayers—a collection which, unfortunately, we know only through a sketchy description of it in the margins of another late fourteenth-century collection (R). It is there named the "Epitaph of Dom Stefano, Carthusian."

THE "EPITAPH OF STEFANO MACONI" (E)

In the margins of the above-mentioned manuscript, someone has added notes beside each prayer concerning its date, place, and sometimes other circumstances, and mentioning consistently the existence of each, either in Latin or in Italian, in a certain *Epitaphium domini Stephani Cartusiensis* ("Epitaph, or funeral oration, of Dom Stefano, Carthusian," i.e., Stefano Maconi, who joined that order after Catherine's death). Robert Fawtier, following Julien Luchaire, held that it was Caffarini—Maconi's friend since boyhood—who penned these notes in 1398, just eighteen years after Catherine's death.[7] Whoever the author of the notes may have been, they permit us, by their indication of the language and page of each prayer, to reconstruct at least the basic composition if not the text of the "Epitaph." And by far the most interesting factor brought out by such a reconstruction is that, of the twenty-two prayers said to exist in the "Epitaph,"[8] fifteen are said to be in Italian, and only seven in Latin—of which six are the same that have no Italian parallels in other known manuscripts. Might we speculate from this that, at least so far as these twenty-two prayers are concerned, the fifteen in Italian were originally recorded in that language, and the other seven in Latin? It seems not entirely improbable.

The notes in R concerning the "Epitaph" are interesting from another point of view as well. Their pagination begins with 141. What then filled the first one hundred and forty leaves? Fawtier speculates that it may well have been Stefano Maconi's transcription of the *Dialogue,* of which a copy exists in the *Biblioteca Comunale* of Siena comprising exactly one hundred and thirty-eight leaves. If the "Epitaph" was indeed composed of Catherine's *Dialogue* and a collection of her prayers, Maconi did well in calling it an "Epitaph," for he could aptly have considered Catherine's own works to be the best possible "funeral oration" for her. Was he perhaps recalling Giovanni Tantucci's vain attempt to deliver such an oration for Catherine over the din of the miracle-seeking crowd the day of her burial? Tantucci had finally simply said, "You can see that I am incapable of preaching about this maiden; but never mind: she herself preaches about herself most adequately."[9]

If only this "Epitaph" could again see the light of day (assuming that it may still exist in some obscure and uncatalogued library), we might be nearer than we are now to these prayers just as Catherine prayed them, and the textual inconsistencies that still remain unexplained[10] might be resolved.

EXTANT MANUSCRIPTS OF THE PRAYERS[11]

R = Rome, Archives of the General Curia of the Order of Preachers, Ms. XIV.24 (formerly X.2003):

Probably the oldest extant manuscript of the *Prayers*, this large parchment codex dates to the end of the fourteenth century. Twenty-two of Catherine's prayers occupy thirty-three pages of the whole (cc. 173a–189a). It is in the margins of R that we find the notes which provide the only remaining evidence of the existence of the "Epitaph of Stefano Maconi."

S1 = Siena, *Biblioteca Comunale degl'Intronati*, Ms. T.II.7:

This parchment volume also dates to the late fourteenth century, and contains a number of other works besides the *Prayers*. Of the latter, however, there is this note on an eighteenth-century flyleaf: ". . . and it contains some prayers of the same saint, collected by Fra Bartolomeo di Domenico, one of her confessors and later bishop of Corona—as he himself testifies in the process certified for the saint's canonization. . . ."

The volume as it now exists really consists of two separate codices which were bound together only in the eighteenth century (thus the late date of the flyleaf). The first, S1a, is in Latin and contains the same twenty-two prayers as R, in the same order, cc. 33a–55b. The second, S1b, in Italian, contains seventeen prayers (cc. 161a–180b), all but the last corresponding with the prayers in the Latin series, but in a different order.

The two codices are numbered consecutively. The initial O of the first prayer in each is illuminated with a miniature of Catherine at prayer.

N = Naples, *Biblioteca Nazionale*, XIV.B.40:

N is either contemporary with or just slightly later than R and S1. Less accurate in its spelling than these, it begins the same series of prayers in Latin on c. 118a, but ends about halfway through the twelfth prayer on c. 129.

S2 = Siena, *Biblioteca Comunale degl'Intronati*, Ms. I.VI.14:

This early fifteenth-century paper manuscript contains, among other Catherinian items, ninety-six of Catherine's letters, with the last of which (cc. 129d–142c) are intermingled four prayers in Latin and two in Italian, plus an abridged version of Prayers 1 and 2.

This codex and V are of particular importance because they contain texts not found in any other extant manuscript (cf. Table I).

V = Vienna, *Biblioteca Nazionale, Palatino,* 3514:

Professor Eugenio Dupré-Theseider discovered this late fourteenth-century paper manuscript in 1931. It is earlier than S2 and related to it, for it contains the same prayers interpolated with the same letters (cc. 242–283).

S3 = Siena, *Biblioteca Comunale degl'Intronati,* Ms. T.I.2;

B = Bologna, *Biblioteca Universitaria,* Ms. 1574:

Both of these early fifteenth-century manuscripts are important primarily as codices of Caffarini's *Libellus de Supplemento.* But both contain Prayers 6 and 26 incorporated into their text, and provide the only known Latin version of those two prayers.

SIGNIFICANT PRINTED EDITIONS

In the mid-fifteenth century Johannes Gutenberg invented movable type in Germany, and within fifty years Catherine's works were in print in Italy. The first major edition was the work of Aldo Manuzio (A) of Venice, who in 1500 printed three hundred and fifty-three of Catherine's letters, with an Italian version of twenty-six of her prayers. We do not know what manuscript or manuscripts Manuzio used for his text, but Giuliana Cavallini finds that it often reads very much like a translation from Latin, and not a very faithful or felicitous one at that. Still, it remains the earliest Italian version we have of five of the prayers, and the first to have collected all of the twenty-six prayers that have since constituted a sort of "canon."

In 1707 Girolamo Gigli (G) published a new edition of the *Prayers* as part of the fourth volume of his *Opere di S. Caterina da Siena.* Gigli states that he used Manuzio's edition as the basis for his work, but that he corrected it with the help of Tommaso Buonconti's manuscript (now in the *Biblioteca Comunale* of Siena, Ms. I.VI.14). This manuscript, however, Fawtier points out,[12] contains only four of the prayers, of which one is in Latin. Gigli's edition, according to Cavallini, is superior to Manuzio's— but this is true only so far as the language itself is concerned, in that he restores its Sienese flavor in a number of ways. But he leaves untouched certain inconsistencies of content, which have thus persisted in successive editions as well.

Taurisano's edition of 1920 (T) expanded the collection by adding (in a separate section, however) prayers extracted from the *Dialogue* and the *Legendae,* under the title *Preghiere ed Elevazioni.* I have included this edition in Table I primarily for reference purposes, since Taurisano's numbering is different from the other editions.

THE CRITICAL EDITION

In 1978 Giuliana Cavallini (C) published the first truly critical edition of the now-accepted "canon" of twenty-six prayers, positioning the parallel Italian and Latin texts face to face and noting all significant variants among the manuscripts and chief editions. Her edition thus brought together for the first time all available evidence for the closest possible approximation to these prayers as Catherine actually prayed them, as well as the earliest rubrics describing their circumstances.

Cavallini also assembled and analyzed more thoroughly than anyone before her the evidence for the dating of each of the prayers. For reasons proper to the critical nature of her edition, however, she retained in her presentation of the prayers the order shared by all of the chief Latin collections, and placed the four prayers not included in these at the end of her volume.

Finally, she supplied her edition with a wealth of references to biblical allusions, parallels in Catherine's *Letters* and *Dialogue,* and echoes of Thomistic thought. Thus, in Cavallini's edition Catherine's prayers became accessible as never before in the six hundred years since they were first prayed. It is on this edition that the present translation is based.

THE TRANSLATION

The language and style of Catherine of Siena are a challenge to the translator under the best of textual conditions. The *Prayers,* therefore, with their parallel Italian and Latin versions and their sometimes inexplicable inconsistencies from version to version present even more difficulty than usual. On the basis of internal linguistic evidence which usually points to the Italian as probably more original, I have in general followed that text, indicating in the Textual Notes (Appendix I) any departures from that as well as all instances in which any manuscript varies from the translation in a way which could even slightly affect the meaning. For all of these variants I have relied completely on Cavallini's work, since I have not had access to the manuscripts themselves.

Cavallini's literal preservation of the rubrics of the early manuscripts for critical purposes dictated the preservation of their order as well, as has been mentioned. Cavallini could also assume a degree of previous knowledge of Catherine's life and works in most of her readers. But the present translation is somewhat broader in its purposes, and is directed to a quite different readership. So I have taken advantage both of Cavallini's establishment of the chronology of the prayers and of a presumed need on the part of English-speaking readers for a more detailed historical commentary, and have here presented the prayers in their chronological order, incorporating the information provided by the original rubrics into my own introductory notes to each prayer. This makes it possible to set each into its context within Catherine's life, and the whole series into the context of her growth toward the full blossoming of her spirituality in the total giving of her life for the Church she so loved.

As in my translation of the *Dialogue,* I have tried to render Catherine's meaning and style as faithfully as possible in *equivalent* English. Here as there that has meant some breaking down and simplifying of her typically long and complex sentences. And here as there I have taken the liberty to correct obvious inconsistencies of grammar (not as frequent as in the *Dialogue*), and to use inclusive pronouns even where Catherine uses the so-called "inclusive masculine." I have not always followed Cavallini's paragraph divisions, but have divided the text as the flow of the English seemed to dictate.

In the manuscripts and in all editions known to me the prayers are presented in a running fashion, broken up only by the editors' paragraphing. I have found the visual impact of this to be an impression of almost unbearable density and an obstacle to meditative reading. The prayers are intense—even more intense than most parts of the *Letters* and *Dialogue.* Yet, if my imagination extrapolates rightly from what scant descriptive rubrics we have, Catherine's words probably formed themselves in a somewhat irregular rhythm, punctuated by long silences—quite unlike the torrent of her normal dictation style. I have, therefore, presented these prayers in a freer format, dividing the lines thought by thought, as it were, in the hope that this may lead the reader more easily into their spirit.

Most of the biblical references I have noted are the same that Cavallini has pointed out in her edition. In general I have cited their translation according to the *New American Bible.* In some instances, however, the sense of the allusion is lost unless one is aware of the text as it occurs in the Latin *Vulgate,* the only version known to Catherine, and in these cases I have translated the text directly from that version, so indicating it in the note.

I have relied heavily on Cavallini's references to parallels in Catherine's *Letters* and *Dialogue,* though I have added some of my own. Citations from the *Letters* are translated from the critical edition of Eugenio

Dupré-Theseider when they fall within the one volume of that edition so far published, and otherwise from the Tommaseo-Misciattelli edition. Letters are referred to first by the number assigned them in Tommaseo-Misciattelli and then, in parentheses, by the number, if any, assigned them by Dupré-Theseider. *Dialogue* references are all cited from my translation of that work published by Paulist Press.

A major scholarly contribution of Cavallini's edition was her indication of parallels between Catherine's thought and that of Thomas Aquinas, whose theology certainly influenced Catherine's own, probably to the greatest extent through her contacts with other learned Dominicans. Anyone seriously interested in pursuing these parallels would have to consult more than very brief citations, and therefore I have given only the references indicated by Cavallini without, in most cases, including any of the text in question.

I have seldom translated Cavallini's commentaries word for word, but wherever I have drawn on hers as the basis for my own, I have so indicated. The one exception to this explicit recognition is the assignment of date and place for each prayer, in which I have followed her arguments and conclusions consistently.

It must be obvious by now that without the research so competently done by Giuliana Cavallini, this volume as it is would hardly have been possible. For this, for her constant personal encouragement along the way, and for her most thorough and kind review and correction of the manuscript, I thank her. Thanks are due also to my Dominican congregation of Racine, Wisconsin, and in a very special way to Sister Denise Frohmader for many evenings and weekends of critical listening and proofreading.

Here, then, are these twenty-six prayers of Catherine for the first time in English. They are not the sort of prayers one would "recite" as one might the prayers in most prayer books. Rather they are prayers to ponder and to live in the presence of—as did those who first heard and recorded them—so that by entering into the spirit of the one who prayed them, we may find new depth and warmth and honesty for our own prayer. Such is my wish and my prayer for every person who will use this book.

Suzanne Noffke, O.P.

The Prayers of Catherine of Siena

Table I[13]

Occurrence and Sequence of the Prayers in Various Sources

P	E	Latin Manuscripts					Ital.	Mixed	Printed Editions			
		Sla	R	N	S3	B	Slb	S2,V	A	G	T	C
1	15(It)	1	1	1			9	1(It)	I	I	I	I
2	16(It)	2	2	2			10	2(It)	I	II	I	II
1–2								7–8(It)				I–II
3	1(L)	3	3	3					II	III	II	III
4								3(L)	XXII	XXIII	III	XXIII
5							17	5(L)	XXIV	XXV	IV	XXIV
6					f.6b	f.3a		6(It)	III	IV		XXV
7	2(L)	5	5	5					V	VI	V	V
8	3(L)	6	6	6					XVIII	XIX	VI	VI
9	12(It)	19	19				6		XV	XVI	VII	XIX
10	13(It)	20	20				7		XVI	XVII	VIII	XX
11	14(It)	21	21				8		XVII	XVIII	IX	XXI
12	17(It)	22	22				11		XXIII	XXIV	XVIII	XXII
13	18(It)	4	4	4			12		IV	V	X	IV
14	19(It)	7	7	7			13		VI	VII	XI	VII
15	20(It)	8	8	8			14		VII	VIII	XII	VIII
16	21(It)	9	9	9			15		VIII	IX	XIII	IX
17	22(It)	10	10	10			16		IX	X	XIV	X
18	7(It)	11	11	11			1		X	XI	XV	XI
19	5(L)	12	12	12 (inc.)					XIX	XX	XVI	XII
20	6(L)	13	13						XX	XXI	XVII	XIII
21	8(L)	15	15				2		XI	XII	XX	XV
22	11(It)	17	17				5		XIV	XV	XIX	XVII
23	10(It)	16	16				4		XIII	XIV	XXII	XVI
24	9(It)	18	18				3		XII	XIII	XXI	XVIII
25	4(L)	14	14						XXI	XXIII	XXIII	XIV
26					f.117	f.43d		4(It)	XXV	XXVI	XXIV	XXVI

NOTES

1. The first biography of Catherine, written by her closest friend and confidant, was newly translated in 1980 by Conleth Kearns as *The Life of Catherine of Siena.* All subsequent references are to this translation, designated *Life.* For full data on this and all sources, see Bibliography.

2. This Fra Tommaso di Antonio (or Nacci), or simply Tommaso da Siena, is much more generally known as Tommaso Caffarini. This was probably not his true surname, but was attributed to him early in the fifteenth century. Since, however, it is more familiar, I have usually referred to him by this name. The works referred to are his *Libellus de Supplemento Legende Prolixe Virginis Beate Catherine de Senis* and *S. Catharinae Senensis Legenda Minor.*

3. Collected in Vol. VI of the Tommaseo-Misciattelli edition of Catherine's *Letters.*

4. *Il Processo Castellano.*

5. The *Dialogue* was composed by Catherine between Advent of 1377 and October of 1378. She called it "my book," and saw it as her attempt to communicate to others her own vision of the truth concerning the journey of the human soul and the Church to God. In the Introduction to my translation of the *Dialogue* (Paulist Press, 1980) Catherine's life is dealt with in more detail than here.

6. The prayers from the other sources mentioned, except the *Legendae* of Raymond and Caffarini, have been gathered into a single volume by an anonymous "Cateriniano" under the title *Tutte le Preghiere ed Elevazioni di S. Caterina, Dottore della Chiesa.* Those reported in the *Legendae* were collected by Innocenzo Taurisano in *S. Caterina da Siena: Preghiere ed Elevazioni,* 1920 edition.

7. *Sources Hagiographiques,* p. 110; Julien Luchaire, *Mélanges d'Archéologie et d'Histoire,* 1899, t. XIX, p. 156.

8. There may have been more, but there are only twenty-two in the Latin collection to which the notes are added.

9. *Libellus de Supplemento* III, vi, iv, p. 386.

10. These are indicated in the Textual Notes, Appendix I.

11. The abbreviations given here will be used throughout this volume to refer to these manuscripts and printed editions of the *Prayers.*

12. *Oeuvres,* p. 352.

13. Table I is adapted from data assembled by Cavallini in Tables 1–3 (pp. xxi–xxv) and in the introductory matter for each of the prayers in her edition. Numbers under P are the numbers assigned to the prayers in this translation, and represent the chronological order as established by Cavallini. Numbers under each of the manuscripts indicate the sequence in which the prayers occur in each, and where the language of the manuscripts is mixed (E, S2, V) the language of each prayer is given. For the printed editions, the numbers given are those assigned by the respective editors. Note that the twelfth prayer in N is incomplete.

ABBREVIATIONS AND SYMBOLS

P.	Prayer (numbers refer to this translation unless otherwise specified).
Dial.	*Dialogue* (first number refers to chapter; page number given as in translation by Noffke).
Let.	Letter (Tommaseo number given first, followed by Dupré-Theseider number in parentheses where pertinent).
Life	Raymond of Capua's *Legenda Major* (first numbers refer to part and chapter; page numbers given as in translation by Kearns).
S. Th.	*Summa Theologica* of St. Thomas Aquinas.
/	"instead of."
[ ]	"omitted."
Lit.	Literally.

Symbols for manuscripts and printed editions are as noted in *Introduction*.

PRAYERS 1 AND 2

Vigil of the Assumption, August 14, 1376.
At Avignon.

Since 1309, with one brief interlude, the papacy had been in self-imposed exile in Avignon, France, a situation that was contributing greatly to tensions between ecclesiastical authorities and the independent republics of the Italian peninsula, and threatening the unity of the Church. The return of Pope Gregory XI to Rome was one of several purposes that compelled Catherine to travel to Avignon in 1376. She arrived there on June 18[1] with a number of her disciples, having sent Raymond of Capua and others on ahead from Florence, where she had been pleading for that city's reconciliation with the Pope.

Besides whatever personal meetings Catherine had with Gregory during her three-month stay in Avignon (the number and the details are uncertain), she communicated with him several times by letter as well. In Letter 233 (LXXVI), which Dupré-Theseider dates in July or August of that year, Catherine alludes to the Pope's having asked for her prayers:

> My father, brother Raymond, told me on your behalf that I should pray to God, asking whether anything would stand in your way. I have already prayed about it, before and after Holy Communion, and I saw neither death nor any danger. . . .

Prayers 1 and 2—which should really be read as a unity—represent one of certainly many occasions on which Catherine prayed for Gregory, something she surely would have done whether explicitly asked or not, for she always very spontaneously included in her prayers those about whom she was concerned, and for whom was she more concerned than the Pope?

The introductory rubric of R² tells us that Catherine "made this prayer in Avignon just after Pope Gregory XI had commanded her to pray especially for him." A and G specify further that Gregory "had sent word for her to pray to God for him especially in the morning." S2 and V, with a second, abridged, version of the two prayers,[3] give the date as "the vigil of the Assumption of Blessed Mary, in the year of the Lord 1376," and the precise place as "the home of Sir John of Regius, before the chapel altar."

It was not unusual for Catherine to be surrounded by her friends and disciples—and sometimes her enemies—when she prayed. This occasion, according to a postscript to the same abridged version, was no exception. Fra Giovanni Tantucci was there, an Augustinian hermit and theologian from Lecceto, near Siena, who would four years later deliver Catherine's funeral eulogy. Fra Felice di Massa, of the same community, was with him. There was Tommaso Petra, at that time one of Pope Gregory's notaries and afterward secretary to Pope Urban VI. He had met Catherine for the first time in Avignon, and by the time they would meet again in Rome would be her close friend and disciple. There was Gherardo Buonconti, in whose home Catherine had lived during her year in Pisa (1375), and his brother Francesco. Two of her secretaries, Neri di Landoccio Pagliaresi and Stefano Maconi, were there, as well as another fellow-Sienese, Niccolò di Mino Cicerchia. There were three of her host's associates and a number of others, including a certain Fra Giuggione, who had come with Catherine from Florence.

We are seldom told who was responsible for writing down a given prayer as Catherine prayed it, but in this case there are two claimants to the distinction. According to R, G, and A, it was Tommaso Petra. This seems to be supported by the above-mentioned postscript, where Tommaso refers to himself in the first person. But in the longer version in S2 and V, Raymond of Capua is credited with having "collected" Prayer 1, and, in V, Prayer 2 as well. Possibly both men took down the two prayers, but if such is the case it is somewhat strange that Raymond is not mentioned in the long list of witnesses, unless his presence was so constant that it was taken for granted.

Though the narrative testimonies of Catherine's contemporaries supply many descriptions of the saint at prayer, the abridged version of Prayers 1 and 2 provides one of very few instances of such description in the specific collections of the *Prayers:*

> She was rapt beyond her senses, lying completely immobile,
> with her limbs so clasped to her body that they might sooner

have been broken than straightened, and if one limb was moved, her whole body would move. Her eyes were half open.

The break between the two prayers is accounted for thus:

> After this she was silent, lying quiet, absorbed, and motionless as before for an hour or so. And then, still lying that way, she answered the responses she had received to what she had said earlier, in the same sort of abstraction.

And at the end of the two recorded prayers

> she remained as before: silent, motionless, quiet, and absorbed, with her hands spread out and her arms in the form of a cross for an hour or so. Afterwards, holy water was sprinkled on her face and Jesus Christ was invoked over and over. Someone touched her firmly. In a short while the breath began to beat in her and she said several times in a subdued voice, "Praise to God now and always!" And then, as her breath became stronger, she began to speak more clearly and got up praising and blessing God. She did not know what time it was.

PRAYER 1

Godhead!
Godhead!
Ineffable Godhead!
O supreme goodness
that for love alone made us in your image and likeness!   5
For when you created humankind
you did not say (as when you created the other creatures),
"Let it be made."
No, you said—O unutterable love!—
"Let us make humankind in our image and likeness,"[4]   10
so that in this the whole Trinity might give assent together,
and in the powers of our soul
you fashioned us after the very Trinity,
Godhead eternal.
To fashion us after yourself, eternal Father—   15
you who as Father hold and keep all things within yourself—
you gave us memory
to hold and keep what our understanding perceives and knows
of you, infinite goodness.
And in knowing,   20
our understanding shares in the wisdom
of your only-begotten Son.
You gave us our will, gentle mercy, Holy Spirit,
which like a hand reaches up[5]
filled with your love   25
to take whatever our understanding knows
of your unutterable goodness;
and then this will,
this strong hand of love,
fills our memory and affection with you.[6]   30

Thanks, thanks be to you, high eternal Godhead,
that you have shown us such great love
by fashioning us with these gracious powers in our soul:
understanding to know you;
memory to keep you in mind,   35

to hold you within ourselves;
will and love to love you more than anything else.
It is only reasonable
that I should love you, infinite goodness,
once I know you.   40
And so powerful is this love
that neither demon nor anyone else can take it away from us
unless we so will.
How ashamed they should be, then,
who do not love you   45
though they see how much you have loved them!

O eternal Godhead,
ineffable love,
in you I see the love that compelled you
to open the eye of your compassion[7]   50
upon us poor wretches.
For after we had
through our wretchedness and weakness
fallen into the filth of sin
when our first father disobeyed you,[8]   55
you, high eternal Father,
sent us the Word incarnate, your only-begotten Son,
veiled in our poor flesh
and clothed in our mortality.[9]
And you, Jesus Christ,   60
our reconciler,
our refashioner,
our redeemer—
you, Word and love,
were made our mediator.   65
You turned our great war with God
into a great peace.
You took out on your own body
the punishment for Adam's disobedience and our sins
by being obedient   70
even to the shameful death of the cross.[10]
On the cross,
Jesus gentle love,
when you took on your very self
the punishment for the offense committed against your Father,   75

you dealt a blow
that at the same time made amends
for the offense against your Father
and atoned for our sin.[11]

I have sinned against the Lord.   80
Have mercy on me![12]

In whatever direction I turn
I find unutterable love.[13]
So we can never be excused for not loving you,
for it is you alone,   85
God and human,
who loved me without my having loved you,
for I did not exist
and you made me.[14]
Whatever I want to love,   90
whatever has being,
I find in you—
but not sin,
which is non-being and does not exist in you,
and so is not worthy of love.[15]   95
If it is God I want to love
I have your ineffable Godhead,
and if it is humanity I want to love,
you are a man
in whom I can come to know you, priceless purity.   100
If it is a lord I want to love,
you are Lord,
and you paid the price of your blood
when you rescued us from the slavery of sin.[16]
You, eternal Godhead,   105
in your boundless kindness and charity
are lord and father and brother to us.
This Word, your Son,
knowing and accomplishing your will,
was willing to shed his precious blood for our wretchedness   110
on the saving wood of the most holy cross.
You, Godhead, highest wisdom—

I am a foolish and wretched creature
while you are supreme eternal goodness.
I am death   *115*
and you are life.
I am darkness
and you are light.
I am ignorance
and you are wisdom.   *120*
You are infinite
and I am finite.
I am sick
and you are the doctor.
I am a weak sinner who have never loved you.   *125*
You are purest beauty
and I am the filthiest of creatures.[17]
You have drawn me to yourself in unutterable love,
and you draw all of us to yourself
not because you must   *130*
but freely—[18]
if only we choose to let ourselves be drawn to you,
that is, if our will does not rebel against yours.

Woe is me!
I have sinned against the Lord.   *135*
Have mercy on me!

Eternal goodness,
do not look at the wretched deeds we have committed
of our very own selves,
cutting ourselves off from your boundless goodness   *140*
and cutting our souls off from their proper goal.
No, I beg you,
in your infinite mercy
open the eye of your supreme clemency and compassion
and look at your one bride.[19]   *145*
Open the eye of your vicar on earth,
so that he may not love you for his own sake,
nor himself for his own sake,
but may love you for yourself and himself for your sake.

For when he loves either you or himself for his own sake   *150*
we are all lost,
because he who should be our life is our death
to the extent that he is not careful
to shelter us little sheep who are going astray.[20]
But if he loves himself for your sake   *155*
and you for yourself,
we live,
because we receive our example for living
from the good shepherd.[21]

O supreme and ineffable Godhead,   *160*
I have sinned
and am not worthy to pray to you,
but you can make me worthy.[22]
Punish my sins, my Lord,
and do not look at my wretched deeds.   *165*
I have one body,
and to you I offer and return it.
Here is my flesh;
here is my blood;
let me be slain, reduced to nothing;   *170*
let my bones be split apart
for those for whom I am praying,
if such is your will.
Let my bones and marrow be ground up
for your vicar on earth, your bride's only spouse.   *175*
For him I beg you to deign to listen to me.
Let this vicar of yours be attentive to your will,
let him love it and do it,
so that we may not be lost.

Make him a new heart,[23]   *180*
that he may constantly grow in grace
and be strong in raising the standard of the most holy cross[24]
to make the unbelievers share as we do
in the fruit of the passion and blood
of your only-begotten Son,   *185*
the spotless Lamb,
high, eternal, ineffable Godhead.

I have sinned against the Lord.
Have mercy on me!

NOTES

1. Let. 232 (LXXV): "We arrived here in Avignon on June 18, 1376."

2. Throughout these notes the various manuscripts and editions of the *Prayers* will be referred to by their symbols as indicated in the Introduction.

3. This abridged version is found only in Italian, with its rubrics in Latin, and only in S2 and V. For purposes of comparison it is given in this volume after the longer version of Prayers 1 and 2. There, however, the descriptive rubrics are indicated only by ellipses, since they are reported practically in their entirety here.

4. Gn. 1, 3ff.

5. The image of the hand expresses the will's particular function, which is to take hold with free choice of the object presented to it by understanding. The use of this image here reinforces the analogy of the soul's third power with the third Person of the Trinity, to whom Catherine often attributes the function of a hand. Cf. Let. 129 (XXVIIII): "He is the hand who supports the whole world"; and Let. 183 (LVI): "Neither demon nor any other creature can force the will . . . a hand so strong that no enemy is strong enough to withstand it when it is armed with the two-edged knife of hate and love." (Cavallini)

6. Cf. *Dial.* 13, p. 49: "You, eternal Father, gave us memory to hold your gifts and share your power. You gave us understanding so that, seeing your goodness, we might share the wisdom of your only-begotten Son. And you gave us free will to love what our understanding sees and knows of your truth, and so share the mercy of your Holy Spirit." For the interaction of the three powers, cf. *Dial.* 51, pp. 103–104.

7. Catherine speaks often in the *Dialogue* of God's eyes as compassionate and merciful. Cf. the opening lines of ch. 14, 51, 98, 109, 135, 154. Cf. also 2 Chr. 6, 40; Neh. 1, 6; Ps. 33, 18; 34, 15.

8. Cf. *Dial.* 150, p. 330: ". . . you must walk, not sit—walk along the way of my Truth's teaching and not sit down by setting your heart on finite things as do those fools who follow the old man, their first father. They do what he did, for he threw the key of obedience into the filthy mire. . . ."

9. Cf. Phil. 2, 7–8.

10. Cf. Is. 53, 5; 2 Cor. 5, 18–19; Phil. 2, 8; Col. 1, 21–22; 1 Tim. 2, 5; *Dial.* 26, p. 65: "I made of him an anvil where this child of humankind could be hammered into an instrument to release humankind from death and restore it to the life of grace."

11. Cf. Let. 223: "O dear fire of love! You dealt one blow that at the same time took out the punishment of sin on yourself . . . and placated your Father's anger. . . . Thus did you turn the great war into peace." Also *Dial.* 13, p. 50:

"But stirred by the same fire that made you create us, you decided to give this warring human race a way to reconciliation, bringing great peace out of our war."

12. Cf. 2 Sm. 12, 13; Ps. 51, 1. This invocation, which occurs very frequently in the *Prayers,* is almost always in Latin, even within the Italian text. It must surely have been a favorite refrain of Catherine's from the Latin Office (the Liturgy of the Hours).

13. *Dial.* 30, p. 72: "For wherever I turn my thoughts I find nothing but mercy!"

14. Cf. *Dial.* 4, p. 29: ". . . even your own existence comes not from yourself but from me, for I loved you before you came into being." In Let. 204 (V) Catherine invites Bartolomeo Dominici to "look at the ineffable eye of divine charity with which God looked on his creature before he created us, and with which he looks on us still. After he had looked upon us within his very self he fell so boundlessly in love with us that for love he created us."

15. Cf. *Dial.* 47, p. 97: "After all, everything is good and perfect, created by me, Goodness itself." 136, p. 281: "I created and made everything in my goodness, because I am who I am and without me nothing has been made—except sin, which is nothingness." 18, p. 56: "I am the Creator of everything that has any share in being. But sin is not of my making, for sin is non-being. Sin is unworthy of any love, then, because it has no part in me."

16. Cf. Gal. 5, 1: "It was for liberty that Christ freed us. So stand firm, and do not take on yourselves the yoke of slavery a second time!"

17. Cf. *Dial.* 167, p. 364: "You, Light, have disregarded my darksomeness; you, Life, have not considered that I am death; nor you, Doctor, considered these grave weaknesses of mine. You, eternal Purity, have disregarded my wretched filthiness; you who are infinite have overlooked the fact that I am finite, and you, Wisdom, the fact that I am foolishness."

18. Cf. Jn. 6, 44.

19. Cf. Ps. 86, 16: "Turn toward me, and have pity on me." Also *Dial.* 13, p. 49, where Catherine introduces her prayer for the Church: "My Lord, turn the eye of your mercy on your people and on your mystic body, holy Church."

20. Cf. Is. 53, 6: "We had all gone astray like sheep"; also *Dial.* 129, p. 255ff.

21. Cf. 1 Tim. 4, 12: ". . . be a continuing example of love, faith, and purity to believers." 1 Pt. 5, 3–4: "Be examples to the flock . . . so that when the chief Shepherd appears you will win for yourselves the unfading crown of glory."

22. Cf. *Life,* II, i, p. 117: "Do you think that I lack the knowledge or the power to choose the manner in which what I have decreed and planned is to be carried out?"

23. Cf. Ez. 36, 26.

24. For Catherine, "raising the standard of the most holy cross" meant proclaiming a Crusade. Though today we may well question at least some of her reasoning in this regard, she did vigorously support such a venture, and this for several ends: to bring about peace in the Church by uniting feuding Christian

warriors against a common enemy; to prevent the Moslems' pushing their advance into Christian lands; to share the effects of redemption with the unbelievers; to see these converts injected as a renewing force of vitality into an ailing Church. Cf. Let. 218 (LXXIIII), written to Gregory XI during Catherine's stay in Avignon, urging him to proclaim such a Crusade.

PRAYER 2

Prayer 2 is actually a continuation, after a break of "an hour or so," of the previous prayer.

Picking up the theme of God's will, touched on in Prayer 1, Catherine recalls one of her favorite images, that of the fish in the sea and the sea in the fish. The image apparently first rose out of an experience Raymond of Capua tells us took place on August 18, 1370:

> It began when, taking her cue from the priest as he held the Sacrament in his hand, she said the words "Lord, I am not worthy that you should enter into my body"; for as she did so she heard a voice saying to her: "But I am worthy that you should enter into me."
>
> Then, when she had received the Sacrament, she felt her soul enter into God, and God into her soul, in the same way as a fish in the sea is in the water, and the water is in the fish.[1]

PRAYER 2

Godhead!
Godhead!
Eternal Godhead!
I proclaim and do not deny it:
you are a peaceful sea 5
in which the soul feeds and is nourished[2]
as she rests in you
in love's affection and union[3]
by conforming her will with your high eternal will—
that will which wants nothing other 10
than that we be made holy.[4]
So the soul who considers this
strips herself of her own will
and clothes herself in yours.

O most gentle love, 15
it seems to me you are showing
that the truest sign people are dwelling in you
is that they follow your will
not in their own way
but in your way. 20
This is the surest sign that people are clothed in your will:
that they see the cause of events in your will
not in human will,
and that they rejoice
not in material prosperity 25
but in adversity,
which they see as given by your will
and motivated only by love.[5]
So they love adversity
just as they love all the things you have created, 30
all of which are good and therefore worthy of love.
But sin is not from you
and is therefore not worthy of love.
And I, miserable wretch,
have sinned by loving sin.[6] 35

I have sinned against the Lord.
Have mercy on me!
Punish my sins, my Lord.
Purify me,
eternal goodness, ineffable Godhead.   40
Listen to your servant;
do not look at my great many sins.[7]

I beg you to guide toward yourself
the heart and will of the ministers of holy Church, your bride,
so that they may follow you,   45
the slain Lamb,
poor, humble, and meek,
along the way of the most holy cross—
in your way, not their own.[8]
Let them be angelic creatures,   50
earthly angels in this life,[9]
for they must administer the body and blood
of your only-begotten Son, the spotless Lamb.
Let them not be senseless beasts,
for beasts are irrational and are not worthy of this.[10]   55
Bring them together now
and wash them, divine compassion,
in the calm sea of your goodness,
so that they may not dawdle any longer,
losing what time they do have   60
for the time they do not have.[11]

I have sinned against the Lord.
Have mercy on me!

Listen to your servant;
wretched as I am I beg you   65
to hear my voice crying out to you,[12]
most compassionate Father.
I pray to you also
for all the children you have given me
to love with a special love   70

through your boundless charity,
most high, eternal, ineffable Godhead.
Amen.

NOTES

1. *Life*, II, vi, p. 183; also *Dial.* 2, p. 27; 112, p. 211.

2. Cf. *Dial.* 89, p. 163: "She takes her rest then in me, the peaceful sea. Her heart is united with me in affectionate love. . . . When she feels the presence of my eternal Godhead she begins to shed tears that are truly a milk that nourishes the soul in true patience." The Latin text substitutes *velut pisces* for the Italian *si pasce,* probably in analogy to passages such as *Dial.* 2, p. 27: "For then the soul is in God and God in the soul, just as the fish is in the sea and the sea in the fish." (Cavallini)

3. "Affection" is for Catherine the innate tendency that moves us to love, whereas "union" is the fruit of willing assent to love in its highest perfection. (Cavallini)

4. 1 Thes. 4, 3. This is a frequent refrain in all of Catherine's writings.

5. Cf. *Dial.* 99, p. 187f.

6. Cf. *Let.* 30 (I): "Supreme Truth spoke thus to a useless servant of his: 'I want you to be a lover of all things, because all of them are good and perfect and worthy of love, and they were all made by me, supreme goodness—except sin. Sin is not in me, for if it were in me, my dearest daughter, it would be worthy of love.' " Also 1 Tim. 4, 4: "Everything God created is good; nothing is to be rejected when it is received with thanksgiving."

7. Cf. Ps. 51, 11: "Turn away your face from my sins."

8. The object of the previous prayer was the head of the Church; now Catherine extends the same petitions to all the Church's ministers. (Cavallini)

9. Cf. *Dial.* 113, p. 212: "No angel has this dignity, but I have given it to those men whom I have chosen to be my ministers. I have sent them like angels, and they ought to be earthly angels in this life."

10. Cf. *Dial.* 126, p. 245: "O dearest daughter! How they have debased the flesh that was exalted above all the choirs of angels through the union of my divinity with your humanity! O despicable wretched man, not man but beast!"

11. Cf. *Let.* 222: "The soul who considers the truth in the light does not persist in sleeping. No, she rouses herself from slumber and searches with great care for the manner and the path, the place and the time to act. She does not trust in being able to wait for tomorrow, for she sees that she cannot be certain of having tomorrow."

12. Ps. 27, 7: "Hear, O Lord, the sound of my call."

PRAYERS 1 AND 2 (ABRIDGED VERSION)

. . . .

Godhead!
Godhead!
Ineffable Godhead and highest goodness,
who for love alone made us in your image and likeness!
For you did not say,   5
"Let humankind be made,"
as when you made the other creatures.
No, you said,
"Let us make humankind in our own image and likeness,"
so that the whole Trinity might give assent together.   10
And you fashioned us after the Trinity
in our soul's powers:
understanding to know you,
memory to hold you and keep you in mind,
and you gave us will and love   15
to love you more than anything else.
And this love
neither demon nor any other creature can take way from us
unless we ourselves will it.

And after we   20
in our wretched weakness
had fallen into the filth of sin,
you opened the eye of your compassion
and sent to us poor wretches
your only-begotten Son and Word,   25
veiled in our poor flesh
and clothed in our mortality,
Jesus Christ,
our reconciler,
and refashioner   30
and redeemer.

So if it is God we want to love,
we have his ineffable Godhead;

and if it is a man we want to love,
to know you, priceless purity, through him,   35
we have in his kindness and immeasurable charity
our lord,
our father,
our brother.
And he,   40
in knowing and accomplishing your will,
was willing to shed his precious blood
for our wretchedness
on the saving wood of the most holy cross.

You, Godhead, are highest wisdom,   45
and I am a foolish and wretched creature.
You are supreme eternal goodness,
and I am a frail sick creature,
a sinner who have never loved you.
You are most beautiful purity,   50
and I the filthiest of creatures.
In unspeakable love you drew me out of yourself,
and draw all of us to yourself.

I have sinned against the Lord.
Have mercy on me!   55

Eternal goodness,
do not look at our wretchedness
which is ours through our own doing
because we cut ourselves off from your boundless goodness
and cut our soul off from its proper goal.   60
No, I beg you,
open the eyes of your clemency and compassion
and look at your one bride.
Open the eyes of your vicar on earth,
so that he may not love you for his own sake,   65
nor love himself for his own sake,
but may love you for yourself
and himself for your sake.

For when he loves you or himself for his own sake
we are all lost,   70
because our life and our death rest in him;
but if he loves himself for your sake
and you for yourself,
we live.

O supreme and ineffable Godhead,   75
I have sinned
and am not worthy to pray to you,
but you can make me worthy.
I have sinned against the Lord.
Have mercy on me!   80
Punish my sins, my Lord,
and do not look at the wretched deeds
with which I have offended your majesty.
I have one body:
to you I offer and return it,   85
flesh and blood,
nerves and veins.
Let it be broken and reduced to nothing
for those for whom I am praying,
if such is your will.   90
Let my bones and marrow be ground up
for your vicar on earth,
your bride's only spouse.
For him I beg you to deign to listen to me.
Let him be attentive to your will;   95
let him love it and follow it,
so that we may not be lost.
Make him a new heart, Lord,
with strength to raise the standard of the most holy cross,
so that others may share as we do   100
in the sprinkling of the blood
of your only-begotten Son,
the spotless Lamb
eternal, ineffable, high Godhead.

I have sinned against the Lord.   105
Have mercy on me!

. . . .

Godhead!
Godhead!
Eternal Godhead!
I proclaim and do not deny it: *110*
you are a peaceful sea
in whom every soul is immersed
who conforms her will with your eternal will.
And this is the truest sign people are dwelling in you:
that they follow your will in your way,   *115*
not their own;
and that they judge according to your will,
not according to the will of your creatures;
and that they rejoice
not in material prosperity   *120*
but in adversity,
which comes from your most holy will
just as do all the other things you have created—
all of which are good
and are to be loved.   *125*

But sin is not from you
and is therefore not worthy of love.
I have sinned against the Lord.
Have mercy on me!
Punish my sins, my Lord,   *130*
and purify me,
eternal goodness, ineffable Godhead!
Listen, Lord, to your servant.
Reform and guide the will of your holy bride's ministers,
so that they may follow you in your way,   *135*
not their own.
Let them be angelic creatures,
worthy to administer the body and blood
of your only-begotten Son, the spotless Lamb,
and let them not be senseless beasts.   *140*
Immerse them now, eternal compassion,
in the calm sea of your will,
so that they may not dawdle any longer,

losing what time they have
for the time they do not have.   *145*

I have sinned, Lord!
Have mercy on me,
and listen yet more to your servant
for the sake of all the children you have given me
to love with a special love   *150*
through your boundless charity.
For this I give you thanks,
most high, eternal, ineffable Godhead!

. . . .

PRAYER 3

October, 1376.
At Genoa.

Though Gregory XI had since his election wanted to return the papacy to Rome, it was finally Catherine's insistence that clinched his decision to move. The Pope left Avignon by galley on September 13, 1376. Catherine, for reasons we do not know, did not travel with the papal entourage but set out by land with her own company of disciples, with a small fund provided by Gregory and the Duke of Anjou.

From the outset the journey was anything but pleasant for Gregory, and by the time his galleys reached Genoa on October 18, he and his party were in low spirits indeed. The news that greeted them at their landing was no help. The Florentines were warning the Romans that the Pope's coming would bring only "war and devastation." Rome was in an uproar. The Genoese Doge himself, while cordial, was unwilling to have his people know of Gregory's dealings with the Florentines. The French cardinals with Gregory took advantage of every ominous report to persuade the Pope to return to the peaceful exile of Avignon. A consistory was called to this purpose, and Gregory was wavering.

Tommaso Caffarini[1] tells us that at this point Gregory sought out Catherine, who had arrived in Genoa some time before and was staying at the home of Orietta Scotti. He could not, in propriety, go to her by day because of the constant crowds at the house. So he went at night to beg for her prayer that he might know what course to take. He left heartened by their conversation, and on October 29 the papal galleys continued their journey toward Rome, while Catherine and her party stayed on in Genoa for several weeks more, detained there by the illness of several of her disciples.

Whether Prayer 3 was recorded on the actual night of Gregory's visit or later we do not know. The rubric of R tells us simply that it

> was made in the city of Genoa, to dissuade Pope Gregory from the proposal, already endorsed in consistory, that he should turn back because of the obstacles to his going to Rome.

PRAYER 3

O Father all-powerful,
eternal God,
O boundless most gentle charity!
I see in you
and know in my heart   5
that you are the way, truth, and life[2]
by which everyone must travel
who is destined to come to you—
the way, truth, and life
which your unutterable love establishes and fashions   10
out of the true knowledge
of the wisdom
of your only-begotten Son, our Lord Jesus Christ.[3]
You are the eternal and incomprehensible God[4]
who, when the human race was dead   15
because of our wretched weakness,
were moved only by love
and by merciful compassion
to send us this one,
our true God and Lord,   20
Christ Jesus your Son,[5]
clothed in our mortal flesh.
And it was your will that he should come
not with the pleasures and splendors of this passing world,
but in anxiety, poverty, and anguish,   25
knowing and accomplishing your will,
for our redemption counting as nothing
the world's perils and the enemy's obstructions
so that he might overcome death by dying,[6]
being obedient even to the most bitter death of the cross.[7]   30

And now,
O love incomprehensible,
you yourself are the very one
who are sending your vicar
to buy back the children who are dead   35

because they have cut themselves off
from obedience to holy mother Church, your one bride—
and you send him in anxiety and perils,
just as you sent your beloved Son, our Savior,
to free the same dead children   40
from the penalty of disobedience
and the death of sin.[8]
But your weak human creatures,
with wicked presumptuous judgment and fleshly motivation,[9]
see things otherwise,   45
so that, taken in by the enemy,
they hinder your will and its fruition,
their own salvation,
and divert your vicar on earth
from this saving mission of yours.   50
O love eternal,
these people fear bodily death
but not spiritual death,
and they judge according to their selfish love and sensuality,
not according to your majesty's true judgment   55
and deep wisdom.[10]

You have been set up as our rule,
and you are the door through which we must pass.[11]
Therefore we should rejoice
in toil and deprivation,   60
as you have said.[12]
It is for this we were born,
and by your wonderful providence
the world and our most wretched flesh
produce no fruit but bitterness.   65
So we should neither rejoice nor hope in these,
but rather glory in the fruit of salvation
and in your heavenly gifts.[13]

Your vicar, then, surely ought to rejoice in doing your will
and following the justice of Christ Jesus,[14]   70
who in his unutterable compassion for us
opened up and drained and let go of his most holy body,

and gave his blood
to wash away our sins[15]
and buy back our wholeness.   75
And he gave this vicar of yours the keys
for binding and freeing our souls,[16]
so that he should do your will
and follow in his footsteps.[17]
This is why I pray and beseech your most holy mercy   80
that you so purify him
that his heart may burn with holy desire
to win back your lost members,
so that he may win them back
with the help of your most high power.   85
And if his dallying displeases you,
O love eternal,
punish my body for it,
for I offer and return it to you
to scourge and ravage as you please.   90

My Lord, I have sinned;
have mercy on me!

You, God eternal—
in your mercy and unutterable grace
you have fallen in love with what you have made.[18]   95
So you are sending your vicar to win it back,
for it has been lost,
and for this I, poor unworthy sinner, thank you.
O infinite goodness and boundless charity,
true God,   100
let humankind, Adam's child,
whom you bought back for love alone
by the death of your only-begotten Son,
blush for shame at not having done your will—
you who want nothing other than that we be made holy![19] 105
Eternal God,
in divine charity you made humankind
and for love you became one with us,
and now you are sending us your vicar

to administer to us   *110*
the spiritual graces of our sanctification
and the winning back of these lost children.
Grant that he may do only your will;
let him pay no attention to the counsels of the flesh
that judge according to selfish love and sensuality,   *115*
and let him not be frightened off by any difficulty.
And because everything fails except in you,
most high God,
do not consider my sins as I call out to you,
but in the mercy of your boundless charity   *120*
listen to your servant.

When you parted from us,
you did not leave us orphans
but gave us your vicar,
who gives us the baptism of the Holy Spirit—   *125*
and not only once,
as we were washed once by the baptism of water,
but he is constantly washing us by holy penance
and cleansing us of our sins.[20]
You came to us much abused   *130*
and we, turning away from you,
judge according to the flesh and selfish love.
You are pallid
because your creatures
are constantly throwing your graces away,[21]   *135*
plundering your one bride.
So, eternal compassion,
make your vicar an eater of souls,[22]
ablaze with holy desire for your honor.
Let him cling to you alone,   *140*
for you are high eternal goodness.
Use him to heal our weaknesses;
make your bride whole again
by means of his wholesome counsel and virtuous deeds.
Still more, God eternal,   *145*
reform the lives of these servants of yours
who are present here;
let them follow you the only God
with simple heart and perfect will.[23]

Do not consider my wretchedness   *150*
as I pray to you for them,
but plant them in the garden of your will.[24]
I bless you, O eternal Father,
that you may bless these servants of yours,
so that they may learn to reckon themselves   *155*
as nothing for your sake
and may follow your will,
which alone is purity,
which alone is eternal and everlasting.
And for all of them I give you thanks.   *160*
Amen.

NOTES

1. *Libellus de Supplemento,* II, i, pp. 29–30.

2. Cf. Jn. 14, 6.

3. This "true knowledge" is knowledge of the teaching of Christ crucified, of which God has made a bridge for us. Cf. *Dial.* 29, p. 68ff. (Cavallini)

4. Cf. Rom. 11, 33: "How deep are the riches and the wisdom and the knowledge of God! How inscrutable his judgments, how unsearchable his ways!"

5. Cf. 1 Jn. 4, 10: "Love, then, consists in this: not that we have loved God but that he has loved us and has sent his Son as an offering for our sins." Also Jn. 3, 16: "Yes, God so loved the world that he gave his only Son."

6. Cf. Heb. 2, 14–15: ". . . that by his death he might rob the devil, the prince of death, of his power, and free those who through fear of death had been slaves their whole life long."

7. Cf. Phil. 2, 8: ". . . it was thus that he humbled himself, obediently accepting even death, death on a cross!"

8. Evident here is Catherine's concern for the cities of Tuscany alienated from the papacy—a rift she hoped to see healed through the return of Pope Gregory XI to Rome. (Cavallini)

9. Cf. Rom. 7, 22–23: "My inner self agrees with the law of God, but I see in my body's members another law at war with the law of my mind; this makes me the prisoner of the law of sin in my members."

10. Cf. Jn. 8, 15–16: "You pass judgment according to appearances. . . . Even if I do judge, that judgment of mine is valid because I am not alone: I have at my side the One who sent me."

11. Cf. Jn. 10, 9.

12. Probably a reference to the message of the Sermon on the Mount, especially the Beatitudes. (Cavallini)

13. Cf. *Dial.* 141, p. 289f: "The first world was left bringing forth troublesome thorns so that in all things humankind still finds rebellion. I did not do this

for want of providence or concern for your well-being, but with great providence and concern for your well-being, to take away your trust in the world and make you run straight to me, your goal. Thus the vexation of troubles, if nothing else, will make you raise your heart and will above the world."

14. Cf. Phil. 3, 8–9: "I have accounted all else rubbish so that Christ may be my wealth and I may be in him, not having any justice of my own based on observance of the law. The justice I possess is that which comes through faith in Christ." Also 1 Cor. 1, 30: "He has made him our wisdom and also our justice, our sanctification, and our redemption."

15. Cf. Rv. 1, 5–6: "To him who loves us and freed us from our sins by his own blood . . . —to him be glory and power forever and ever."

16. On the "power of the keys" cf. Mt. 16, 19 and *Dial.* 115, pp. 214f and 155, pp. 329ff.

17. Cf. *Dial.* 75, p. 137: ". . . watch her run across the bridge of the teaching of Christ crucified, who was your rule and way and teaching. It was not me, the Father, that she set before her mind's eye. This is what those do whose love is imperfect. They are not willing to suffer, and since no suffering can befall me, they want to pursue only the pleasure they find in me . . . —not really me, but the pleasure they find in me."

18. Cf. *Dial.* 167, p. 365: "I your handiwork have come to know that you are in love with the beauty of what you have made, since you made of me a new creation in the blood of your Son."

19. Cf. 1 Thes. 4, 3: "It is God's will that you grow in holiness."

20. Cf. Mt. 3, 11: "He it is who will baptize you in the Holy Spirit and fire." Also *Dial.* 75, p. 138: "I know how people sin because of their weakness. . . . So my divine charity had to leave them an ongoing baptism of blood accessible by heartfelt contrition and a holy confession as soon as they can confess to my ministers who hold the key to the blood. This blood the priest pours over the soul in absolution."

21. Cf. Is. 53, 2, 4: "There was in him no stately bearing to make us look at him, nor appearance that would attract us to him. . . . Yet it was our infirmities that he bore, our sufferings that he endured, while we thought of him as one smitten by God and afflicted."

22. "Eating souls" is a favorite Catherinian image for desire for the salvation of others. Those who enter into union with Christ must necessarily share his redemptive love. Cf. *Dial.* 76, p. 140: "She eats the food of souls for my honor at the table of the most holy cross." Also Let. 322: "What is her food? God's honor and the salvation of souls. Once she has risen above seeking her own selfish honor she runs like one in love to the table of the cross to seek God's honor. She fills up on disgrace, embracing insults and abuse, conforming herself entirely to the Word's teaching and in truth follows in his footsteps."

23. Cf. Canon of the Roman Mass: "Remember, Lord, your servants and handmaids . . . and all here present, whose faith and devotion are known to you. . . ."

24. In Prayer 20 the divine mind is called a garden.

PRAYER 4

Feast of the Conversion of St. Paul,
January 25, 1377.
At Siena or Belcaro.

It is thought by some that one of Catherine's reasons for wanting to meet Pope Gregory XI was that she needed his consent to proceed with the realization of her desire to found a cloister for some of her women disciples. She probably obtained that consent while in Avignon, for she had scarcely returned to Siena (near Christmas of 1376) when she approached one of her converts, Nanni di Ser Vanni Savini, and asked him to donate for this purpose the half-ruined fortress of Belcaro, a few miles to the west of Siena. On January 25, 1377, she addressed a petition to the Defenders of the Republic of Siena for authorization to renovate the building, which would become the Monastery of St. Mary of the Angels.

That day was also the feast of the Conversion of St. Paul, and it was on that day, we are told by the rubric in S2 and V, that Catherine prayed the prayer given here and that Raymond of Capua wrote it down. She may have been either at Siena or Belcaro at the time. The rubrics of the Latin text provide a few descriptive details, which I have translated as they occur.

41

PRAYER 4

SHE SAID IN HER RAPTURE AFTER COMMUNION:
O Trinity eternal, one God!
SHE BEGAN WITH THIS FIRST INVOCATION, WHICH,
AS WAS HER CUSTOM, SHE REPEATED MANY TIMES.
AFTER A LITTLE WHILE SHE WENT ON: 5
You,
Godhead,
one in being and three in Persons,
are one vine with three branches—[1]
if I may be permitted to make such a comparison. 10
You made us in your image and likeness so that,
with our three powers in one soul,
we might image your trinity
and your unity.[2]
And as we image, 15
so we may find union:
through our memory,
image and be united with the Father,
to whom is attributed power;
through our understanding, 20
image and be united with the Son,
to whom is attributed wisdom;
through our will,
image and be united with the Holy Spirit,
to whom is attributed mercy, 25
and who is the love
of the Father and the Son.
THEN, TURNING HER ATTENTION TO THE BLESSED
  PAUL, SHE SAID:
You, wonderful Paul, pondered this well,
and so you truly knew 30
where you had come from
and where you were going—[3]
and not only where you were going
but even the road you were traveling,
for you had come to know your origin 35
and your goal

and the road by which you would travel to your goal.
Thus you joined your soul's powers
with the divine Persons.
For you joined your memory with the Father,   40
perfectly mindful that he is the origin
from whom all things come,
and not only created things
but even, in their own way,
the divine Persons themselves.[4]   45
Because of this you never in any way doubted
that he was *your* origin.
You joined your power of understanding with the Son,
the Word,
understanding perfectly the whole order   50
ordained by wisdom itself,
the Word,
the order that is to lead created things to their goal—
and their goal is the same as their origin.[5]
So that such might be more clearly revealed,   55
this Word became flesh
and lived among us.[6]
He, since he is Truth,
would by his actions make himself the way
by which we might travel to the life[7]   60
for which we had been created
but which we had lost.
You joined your will with the Holy Spirit,
loving perfectly that love,
that mercy   65
you knew was the reason for your creation
and for every grace given to you
without your earning it.[8]
And you knew
that divine mercy had done this for one purpose: 70
to make you blessed and happy.

That is why on this day,
after you were converted by the Word himself
from error to truth,[9]
and after you received the gift   75
of being rapt to where you saw the divine Being in three Persons,[10]

once you were deprived of that vision
and returned to your body
(or simply to your senses),
you remained clothed   80
only in the vision of the incarnate Word.
When you considered attentively in this vision
that this very Word incarnate suffered constantly
as he worked out his Father's honor
and our salvation,   85
it made you desirous and thirsty to suffer,[11]
so that, oblivious of all else,
you might proclaim
that you knew nothing but Jesus Christ,
and him crucified.[12]   90
Since no suffering
could befall the Father or the Holy Spirit,
it seems almost as if you forgot about those Persons
and said that you knew only the Son—
and him enduring the most bitter sufferings—   95
for you added,
"and him crucified."

NOTES

1. An original, bold, and apparently unique application to the Trinity of the well-known image of Jn. 15, 5: "I am the vine, you the branches." (Cavallini)

2. Cf. *S. Th.* I, q. 93, a. 5.

3. Cf. Jn. 8, 14: "I know where I came from and where I am going." But Catherine applies these words to the Apostle in the context of the experience that overtook him on the road to Damascus (Acts 9) and gave his spirit a new orientation and his journey a different purpose. (Cavallini)

4. Cf. Eph. 3, 14–15: ". . . the Father from whom every family in heaven and on earth takes its name. . . ."

5. Jn. 8, 25 (Vulgate): "So they said to him, 'Who are you?' Jesus said to them, 'The Beginning, who am speaking to you.' " Also 1 Cor. 15, 22–25: "Just as in Adam all die, so in Christ all will come to life again, but each one in proper order . . . after having destroyed every sovereignty, authority and power, he will hand over the kingdom to God the Father. Christ must reign until God has put all enemies under his feet."

6. Jn. 1, 14.

7. Cf. Jn. 14, 6: "I am the way, and the truth, and the life."

8. 1 Cor. 15, 9–10: "I am the least of the apostles; in fact, because I perse-

cuted the church of God, I do not even deserve the name. But by God's favor I am what I am."

9. Acts 9, 5: " 'Who are you, sir?' . . . 'I am Jesus, the one you are persecuting.' "

10. 2 Cor. 12, 2f.: "I know a man in Christ who . . . was snatched up to the third heaven. . . ."

11. Cf. Col. 2, 24–25: "Even now I find my joy in the suffering I endure for you. In my own flesh I fill up what is lacking in the sufferings of Christ for the sake of his body, the church."

12. 1 Cor. 2, 2: "I determined that while I was with you I would speak of nothing but Jesus Christ and him crucified."

PRAYER 5

October 26, 1377.
At Rocca di Tentennano, Val d'Orcia.

After spending most of April at Belcaro (see Prayer 4), Catherine traveled south about twenty-five miles to the Val d'Orcia, to the fortress of Agnolino Salimbeni at Rocca di Tentennano. There was a feud between Agnolino and his brother Cione to be mediated, and Catherine was intent as well on directing the futures of several widowed Salimbeni women. Rocca d'Orcia lay on the fringes of Sienese territory, and while she prolonged her stay there to preach to the people of the countryside, rumors began flying back in Siena that she and her company were in fact there for suspect political purposes. Catherine found it necessary to defend her loyalty to her city both by letter and by emissary. One such letter (122) was sent to Salvi di Misser Pietro, a goldsmith who had some influence with the ruling party:

> And if they give me persecution and defamation, I will give as much continual prayer and weeping as God gives me grace. And whether the devil wants it or not, I will strive to spend my life for God's honor and the salvation of souls—for the whole world, yes, but especially for my city. The citizens of Siena are doing themselves a shameful disservice by imagining or believing that we are engaged in plotting in the territory of the Salimbeni. . . . They are telling the truth without knowing it, and are prophesying, for the only plotting I want to do, and the only plotting I want anyone with me to do, is to defeat the devil and deprive him of the mastery he has gained over people by deadly sin—to take the hatred out of people's hearts and reconcile them with Christ crucified and with their neighbors. These

46

are the plots we are engaged in and that I want whoever is with
me to be engaged in.

Prayer 5 is not found in any Latin manuscript, and in the Italian
versions there is confusion as to both its time and place. The earliest extant rubric to the prayer (S2, V) places it at Rocca d'Orcia. A and G give
the date as October 26, but differ in the year. The entire context of
Catherine's time at Rocca d'Orcia in 1377 supports correcting to 1377
the 1378 dating given by G (already corrected from A's obviously mistak-
en 1308). Note especially the allusion in lines 14–15 to "my own enemies." Besides, we know that Catherine was in Siena in October of 1378
and, while she certainly could have paid a visit to the Salimbeni at that
time, we have a letter of hers (262), dated October 26, 1378 in at least
one manuscript, which makes no mention of Rocca d'Orcia or its inhabit-
ants.[1]

The prayer is a typically Trinitarian one, calling on the Father as
power, the Son as wisdom, and the Holy Spirit as mercy. Its concerns
reflect Catherine's preoccupations during those fall months in the Val
d'Orcia: peace and unity for the Church (Raymond of Capua had left for
Rome just a few weeks before, carrying "certain proposals which, if only
people had understood, would have been for the advantage of the holy
Church of God"[2]), mercy for the people to whom she was ministering,
and strength for herself in the tension under which she found herself
working.

PRAYER 5

Power of the eternal Father,
help me!
Wisdom of the Son,
enlighten the eye of my understanding!
Tender mercy of the Holy Spirit,   5
enflame my heart
and unite it to yourself!
I proclaim, eternal God,
that your power is powerful and strong enough
to free your Church and your people,[3]   10
to snatch us from the devil's hand,
to stop the persecution of holy Church,
and to give me strength and victory
over my own enemies.[4]
I proclaim that the wisdom of your Son,   15
who is one with you,
can enlighten the eye of my understanding
and that of your people,
and can relieve the darkness of your sweet bride.[5]
And I proclaim, eternal gentle goodness of God,   20
that the mercy of the Holy Spirit,
your blazing charity,
wants to enflame my heart
and everyone's
and unite them with yourself.[6]   25

Power of you, eternal Father;
wisdom of your only-begotten Son
in his precious blood;
mercy of the Holy Spirit,
fire and deep well of charity   30
that held this Son of yours
fixed and nailed to the cross—[7]
you know how to
and you can
and you want to,[8]   35

so I plead with you:
have mercy on the world
and restore the warmth of charity
and peace
and unity   40
to holy Church.
O me!
I wish you would not delay any longer!⁹
I beg you,
let your infinite goodness force you   45
not to close the eye of your mercy!

Gentle Jesus!
Jesus love!

NOTES

1. Cf. R. Fawtier, *Ste. Catherine de Sienne, essaie de critique des sources: les oeuvres de Ste. Catherine de Sienne,* pp. 358–359. Fawtier's conclusion was that the prayer should be dated October 26, 1379, at Rome. He bases his argument on a rubric in R, which he says contains this prayer. Cavallini's description of R, however, states that R contains only 22 prayers, and this one is not among them. I have followed Cavallini's reasoning and conclusions on the matter, since it seems more trustworthy than Fawtier's.

2. *Life,* III, vi. p. 382.

3. Cf. Eph. 3, 20–21: "To him whose power now at work in us can do immeasurably more than we ask or imagine—to him be glory in the church and in Christ Jesus. . . ."

4. Cf. 1 Jn. 5, 4: "Everyone begotten of God conquers the world, and the power that has conquered the world is this faith of ours." Also 1 Cor. 15, 57: "But thanks be to God who has given us the victory through our Lord Jesus Christ."

5. Cf. 2 Tim. 1, 9–10: ". . . the grace held out to us in Christ Jesus before the world began but now made manifest through the appearance of our Savior. He has robbed death of its power and has brought life and immortality into clear light through the gospel." Also 1 Cor. 1, 30: "He has made him our wisdom and also our justice, our sanctification, and our redemption."

6. Cf. Rom. 5, 5: ". . . the love of God has been poured out in our hearts through the Holy Spirit who has been given to us." Also Acts 4, 31–32: "They were filled with the Holy Spirit and . . . were of one heart and one mind."

7. Cf. *S. Th.* III, q. 47, a. 2.

8. Cf. Mk. 1, 40–41: " 'If you will to do so, you can cure me.' Moved with pity, Jesus stretched out his hand, touched him, and said, 'I will do it. Be cured.' "

9. Cf. Ps. 40, 18: "You are my help and my deliverer; O my God, hold not back!"

PRAYER 6

Autumn, 1377.
At Rocca di Tentennano, Val d'Orcia.

At the end of a letter to Raymond of Capua in early October, 1377, Catherine tells—almost as an aside—of God's providence in "giving me the ability to write, so that when I come down from the heights I might have a little something to vent my heart, lest it burst." Her brief description of just how she learned is very cryptic: "In a marvelous manner he fixed it in my mind the way a teacher does when he gives his pupil an example. Shortly after you left me, I began to learn, with the glorious evangelist John and Thomas Aquinas, as if I were sleeping."[1]

This is the context for Prayer 6. Tommaso Caffarini, the only one of Catherine's biographers to report the story, tells us that she happened on a small jar of ink, the sort used for manuscripts, and some pens. Though she had never learned to write, she sat down, took a pen and a small sheet of paper, and wrote this prayer—in her own Tuscan dialect—in the well-formed letters of a practiced scribe. The original, he says, found its way to him after having passed through the hands of at least two others, and was eventually placed in the convent of the Dominican Sisters of Penance in Venice, a convent which, after near-destruction and several changes of jurisdiction, was finally suppressed in 1810. The document has not been recovered.[2]

Probably none of Catherine's prayers has been so frequently cited in English as this one; yet it is also the most disputed. Robert Fawtier rejected its authenticity because "none of the manuscripts that have preserved the text of the Prayers for us contains this one."[3] The prayer is, in fact, in S2, which Fawtier both knew and cited. His rejection was probably more basically motivated by his utter mistrust of Caffarini's credibility. A more serious reservation is raised by Alvaro Grion: the Trinitarian

51

references in the prayer are not at all typical of Catherine, who habitually attributes power to the Father, wisdom to the Son, and mercy to the Holy Spirit. Here power is associated with the Spirit, warmth and love with the Son, and help with the Father.[4]

It is true that the language of this prayer does not in many respects correspond to Catherine's usual style in its vocabulary, its structure, or its approach to the Trinity. Cavallini, who accepts its authenticity, attributes its peculiarities to the stress under which Catherine was living at the time (cf. introduction to Prayer 5):

> In this climate of conflict which perhaps threatens to impair in the depths of her soul her will to love all people always, in spite of everything, it is natural that she should turn first to the Spirit of love, that he might draw her to himself and give her love and fear—and then to Christ, that he might guard her spirit, and to the Father that he might help her in her works. Even if the order is reversed, the attributions to the three Persons are implicit in the petitions directed to each.[5]

Cavallini also points out in her notes other passages from clearly authentic Catherinian writings which contain parallel "inconsistencies" in attributions to the Persons of the Trinity (cf. footnotes), and that St. Paul himself could have been her model in this, e.g., in 1 Cor. 13, 13: "The grace of the Lord Jesus, and the love of God, and the fellowship of the Holy Spirit be with you all!" This, however, still leaves the structural and lexical peculiarities unexplained.

I would turn for a possible explanation to the context of the writing, a context different from that for any other prayer in the collection, and also to the structure of the prayer itself.

We have basically two versions of the prayer, the second (A, G) slightly more expanded than the first (S2, V).[6] Both vocabulary and grammar would seem to suggest that the first is closer to the original, or at least closer to Catherine's usual language. The second and longer version, especially in the Italian, reveals a clear pattern of rhyme and assonance (ABABCCBABA), with a somewhat irregular scansion. Catherine, however, used such poetic devices nowhere else in all her writings. Did the source used by A and G revise the original to produce the more "poetic" form? Or are S2 and V abridged? Did Caffarini make his Latin translation from the original he claims to have had in his possession? If so, the longer version, which is extremely close to Caffarini's Latin in all but rhyme scheme, would stand as nearer the original.

If Caffarini's whole story is indeed true, it seems quite plausible that the prayer is simply one that Catherine knew from memory, a prayer not her own except in the sense that she liked it well enough to have memorized it (with perhaps some not untypical personal adaptations, which could account for the skewed scansion). Besides, the setting Caffarini describes is one in which it would seem far more natural to draw on such a familiar refrain than to compose—especially in an unaccustomed style. This would also account, then, for any inconsistencies with Catherine's normal usage.

Whatever the reality of its origin, the prayer is not alien to Catherine's attitudes, and whether she actually composed it or not, it did come in one way or another to be associated with her. I therefore include it here with no firm judgment of my own as to its originality. I have set it in the ten lines into which the rhyme and assonance pattern divides it, including the elements which are not in the shorter version. Variations between the versions are detailed in the Textual Notes.

PRAYER 6

O Holy Spirit, come into my heart;
by your power draw it to yourself, God,[7]
and give me charity with fear.
Guard me, Christ, from every evil thought,[8]
and so warm and enflame me again   5
with your most gentle love
that every suffering may seem light to me.
My holy Father and my gentle Lord,
help me in my every need.[9]
Christ love! Christ love!   10

NOTES

1. Let. 272.

2. *Il Processo Castellano*, ed. M.-H. Laurent, *Fontes Vitae S. Catharinae Senensis Historici*, IX, pp. 62–63; *Libellus de Supplemento*, I, i (for data on the convent in Venice, see Cavallini's note to the latter, *Libellus*, p. 17).

3. *Oeuvres*, p. 354.

4. *S. Caterina da Siena, dottrina e fonti*, pp. 174–177.

5. *Orazioni*, p. 277.

6. The Latin is Caffarini's translation.

7. Cf. *Dial.* 26, p. 65: ". . . the human heart is always drawn by love." And in Let. 109 (LI) Catherine calls divine charity (which she equates with the Holy Spirit) "a gentle drawing fire." This charity has the divine strength of the Holy Spirit, of whom Catherine writes in Let. 129 (XXVIIII): ". . . for love, that is, the Holy Spirit, sustains everything. . . . In that vein I recall his saying . . . 'I am the one who upholds and sustains the whole world. It was through me that the divine and human natures were united. I am the mighty hand that holds up the standard of the cross. . . .' " (Cavallini)

8. Cf. *Dial.* 124, p. 239: ". . . let your place of refuge be my only-begotten Son, Christ crucified. Make your home and hiding place in the cavern of his open side." There one experiences the love of God and of one's neighbors. In P. 19 this cavern of Christ's side is "a refuge in the face of our enemies." (Cavallini)

9. V has *mestiero* ("occupation" or "need"); A and G have *ministerio* ("ministry" or "service"). Both *mestiero* and *ministerio* come from the same Latin root, *ministerium*, but Caffarini translates (presumably from *mestiero*) *necessitate* ("need" or "obligation"). S2 has *misterio* ("mystery," usually *mistero* in Cather-

ine). Though *mistero* was for Catherine a favorite concept, including in a very sacramental sense every meeting of God with humanity, even in our weakness and sin, I know of no other instance of her speaking of *"my* mystery." It seems most likely, then, that the original text had *mestiero,* which I have translated as "need," since this could embrace ministerial as well as personal concerns. Cavallini: this plea for help presupposes power in the One who is addressed for help.

PRAYER 7

Feast of St. Thomas the Apostle,
December 21, 1378.
At Rome.

The months between the previous prayer and this one were not by
any means empty ones for Catherine. She returned to Siena from Rocca
d'Orcia around Christmas of 1377, but had scarcely settled in there
when Gregory XI sent orders for her to travel to Florence to attempt once
more to mediate a reconciliation of that city, under interdict since
March, 1376, with the papacy. After a turbulent seven months filled
with futility and frustration, the peace was concluded with no apparent
reference to Catherine's efforts, and she returned quietly to Siena.
There she finished her book, *The Dialogue,* which she had been working
on, at least sporadically in the midst of all her other involvements, since
the autumn before.

Gregory XI had died on March 27, while Catherine was still in Florence, and on April 8 Urban VI had been elected to succeed him. The
election itself had been chaotic enough, but soon after, the rumblings of
schism began to be heard as cardinal after cardinal rejected the new Pope
and his often violent reform measures. On September 20 they gathered
in conclave at Fondi and elected Robert, Cardinal of Geneva, to be Pope
in Urban's place. From the beginning Catherine publicly and vocally up-
held Urban's legitimacy, writing in the most uncompromising language
to any she thought she might influence to reverse the schism. In November Urban sent word through Raymond of Capua for Catherine to come
to Rome, for he desperately needed whatever support she could lend to
his cause. She hesitated at first, because people were accusing her of being a gadabout and a meddler; but when the written orders arrived

(which she had requested as a condition of her going), she made her plans and set out.

She and a good number of her disciples arrived in Rome on November 28, and here she would spend the remaining year and a half of her life. Rome, therefore—Rome devastated by schism—is the context for the rest of Catherine's recorded prayers.

Prayer 7, we are informed by a rubric in the margin of R, was prayed "in the time of Pope Urban VI on the feast of St. Thomas the Apostle, in Rome." The year is not given, but though Catherine was in Rome on that feast the following year as well, her references to the "new plants" (the cardinals named by Urban in September, 1378) and to the Pope himself as "this new spouse of the Church" point certainly to 1378. Catherine had been in Rome barely three weeks, then, and the effects of the schism literally engulfed her. Besides, she had once again been separated from Raymond, her dearest friend and confidant, who had been sent off by Urban on a mission to France within days of Catherine's reunion with him. Her whole attention in this prayer is concentrated on the Pope and the new cardinals and the sort of persons they must be if they are to serve as effective instruments of reform in the Church.

PRAYER 7

O Godhead!
Godhead!
Eternal Godhead!
True love!
Through the union of the humanity of your Word,   5
our Lord Jesus Christ,
with your all-powerful Godhead,
you have given to us who were lost
the light of most holy faith,
the pupil of the eye of our understanding,[1]   10
with which we see and know our soul's true goal,
your immeasurable Godhead.[2]
And you have made this Son of yours
a spotless sacrifice for us,
establishing him as the cornerstone[3]   15
and firmest pillar of stability
for holy mother Church,[4]
your one bride.
Long ago you decided to renew this Church
with new and more fruitful plants,   20
and from that time on
no one could break your most holy will,
eternal and unchangeable.

Do not consider our sins,
because of which I know I am unworthy to pray to you.   25
In your most merciful compassion
take away these sins of ours today
through the power of your holy apostle Thomas.
Purify my soul,
most high God, my love,   30
and listen to your servant
who is calling out to you.[5]

You are a fire always burning.
Yet,
though you always consume   35

all that the soul possesses apart from you,
you never consume
the things that are pleasing to you.
Burn with the fire of your Spirit
and consume,   40
root out from the bottom up,
every fleshly love and affection
from the hearts of the new plants[6]
you have kindly seen fit
to set into the mystic body of holy Church.[7]   45
Transplant them
away from worldly affections
into the garden of your own affection,
and give them a new heart
with true knowledge of your will.[8]   50
Make them despise the world
and themselves
and selfish love.
Fill them with your love's true fervor
and make them zealous for faith and virtue.   55
And so,
once they have left behind
the false desires and pretenses
of this passing world,
let them follow you alone   60
in purest purity
and glowing charity.

And then, director of our salvation,[9]
let this new spouse of the Church[10]
be directed always by your counsel.   65
Let him accept
and listen to
and encourage
only those who are clean and pure.
As for these other newest plants of yours,   70
let them stand before our lord your vicar on earth
just as the angels stand before you in heaven,
for the reform of this holy mother Church
after the pattern of your own heart,
with simple heart and perfect work.   75

Let them see themselves for what they are,
newly engrafted in the body of our Lord Jesus Christ—
from which you in your wondrous providence,
without human help,
have cut off certain barren and unneeded branches.[11]   *80*
And just as Jesus himself
is even now being born and progressing in age and virtue,
so let them,
now that they have been born in this same Church,
likewise progress in virtuous ways and example.[12]   *85*
Branches newly engrafted
produce more fragrant blossoms
and more pleasing fruit
because of the natural disposition they have from you.
Just so,   *90*
once the impulses of every fleshly affection
have been cut off by your heavenly gift—[13]
the dew of the Holy Spirit
in which you bathed the holy apostles—[14]
let new virtues be engrafted in them   *95*
which will offer you a sweet fragrance.[15]
And may they themselves offer this holy Church
the pleasure of virtuous deeds and fruitful works,
so that in them your bride may be reformed.

O eternal love,   *100*
purify this vicar of yours
in himself
so that he may give the others a good example
of purity and innocence.
May he serve willingly in your presence.   *105*
May he instruct the people subject to him,
and even attract unbelievers with heavenly teachings,
and offer to your unfathomable majesty
the fruit of [their] eternal salvation.

So that you may deign to listen to these things,   *110*
supreme goodness,
true God,

I, poor as I am,
give you thanks for all of them.
Amen.   *115*

NOTES

1. Cf. *Dial.* 45, p. 92: ". . . they know my truth when their understanding—which is the soul's eye—is enlightened in me. The pupil of this eye is most holy faith, and this light of faith enables them to discern and know and follow the way and teaching of my Truth, the incarnate Word."

2. Though natural reason can know God's nature and attributes in so far as they are reflected in creation (cf. Rom. 1, 20: "Since the creation of the world, invisible realities, God's eternal power and divinity, have become visible, recognized through the things he has made"), and reason enlightened by faith participates in God's own self-knowledge, we cannot in this life know God as he really is; therefore Catherine says that the Godhead is "immeasurable." Cf. 1 Tim. 6, 16: God "dwells in unapproachable light, whom no human being has ever seen or can see." Also St. Thomas Aquinas, *Super Ev. S. Ioannis Lect.* 211. (Cavallini)

3. Cf. Is. 28, 16: "See, I am laying a stone in Zion, a stone that has been tested, a precious cornerstone as a sure foundation; they who put their faith in it shall not be shaken." Eph. 2, 20: "You form a building which rises on the foundation of the apostles and prophets, with Christ Jesus himself as the capstone." (An allusion to a reading for the feast of St. Thomas?)

4. Cf. 1 Tim. 3, 15: ". . . the church of the living God, the pillar and bulwark of truth."

5. Cf. Ps. 141, 1: "O Lord . . . hearken to my voice when I call upon you."

6. Catherine often uses the image of plants in the garden of the Church to refer to the servants of God, but most especially to the hierarchy. Here the reference is certainly to the cardinals named by Urban VI in September of 1378.

7. Cf. *Dial.* 167, p. 365: "You are a fire always burning but never consuming; you are a fire consuming in your heat all the soul's selfish love; you are a fire lifting all chill and giving light." Ex. 3, 2: ". . . the bush, though on fire, was not consumed." Dt. 4, 24: "For the Lord, your God, is a consuming fire, a jealous God."

8. Cf. Ez. 36, 26–27: "I will give you a new heart and place a new spirit within you, taking from your bodies your stony hearts and giving you natural hearts. I will put my spirit within you. . . ."

9. Cf. *Dial.* 135–153, "Divine Providence." In 152, p. 324, we read, "I have done and do all I do in providence for your salvation from the beginning . . . right up to the end."

10. Pope Urban VI, elected only a little more than eight months earlier.

11. Cf. Jn. 15, 2: "He prunes away every barren branch." Rom. 11, 17: "If some of the branches were cut off and you, a branch of the wild olive tree, have been grafted in among the others and have come to share in the rich root of the olive, do not boast against the branches." The new branches are again the new cardinals appointed to replace the schismatics. Cf. Let. 310 to three schismatic Italian cardinals: "You are separated from the vine of grace, members cut off from your head. . . ." (Cavallini)

12. The reference to Christ "being born and progressing in age and virtue" (cf. Lk. 2, 52) reflects the near approach of Christmas as Catherine prayed this prayer. Beyond this, there is some uncertainty as to Catherine's exact meaning in this sentence, since the Italian and Latin texts do not agree. (Cavallini) I have followed the Latin, as it is the older of the two texts from available evidence (the earliest extant Italian copy of this prayer is that of Aldo Manuzio, 1500, and may well be a translation from the Latin, as internal evidence seems to indicate). Also, in this case, the Latin seems to me more Catherinian in tone. The Italian translates: "And they have been born in their old age, with Jesus himself even now being born and progressing in virtue—so let them in this same Church likewise produce fruit in virtuous ways and example."

13. Cf. *Dial.* 45, p. 93: ". . . as far as sensual love is concerned their heart has been drawn away from themselves and is firmly joined to me by the impulse of love."

14. Cf. the hymn *Veni Creator,* where the Holy Spirit is invoked as "gift of God most high," and the Sequence for Pentecost: "Bedew what is dried up." Also Let. 113: "[This divine charity] is a dew and a rain that waters the planted tree and the earth of true humility. It nourishes this earth and the garden of self-knowledge, for now it is seasoned with the knowledge of God's goodness to us." For Catherine as for the Church in its tradition, divine charity and the Holy Spirit are one, so she can well use the same image for both.

15. A frequent biblical image for an offering pleasing to God, e.g., Eph. 5, 2: "Follow the way of love, even as Christ loved you. He gave himself for us as an offering to God, a gift of pleasing fragrance." (Cavallini)

PRAYER 8

Feast of the Chair of St. Peter, January 18, 1379.
At Rome.

On this occasion as on so many others, Catherine's prayer took its theme from the liturgy of the day. One would expect her, though, to have been especially moved by this particular feast, preoccupied as she was with the stormy fortunes of the papacy. Still, there is a note of hope and even optimism in this prayer, for the new year had opened with at least a few good omens. England had declared a firm allegiance to Urban VI; Wenceslaus, King of the Romans, was maintaining his loyalty; and Louis of Hungary and Poland, a powerful force in eastern Europe, was offering hope of military aid in what was becoming an all-out war. On January 1 Catherine had written to Pietro di Giovanni and Stefano Maconi, who were still in Siena (Let. 332):

> Holy Church and Pope Urban VI, by God's tender goodness, have had the most important news they have had in a long time. I am sending you with this a letter for the Bachelor [William of Flete], in which you can see how God is beginning to pour out graces on his dear bride. And so I hope he will continue in his mercy to multiply his gifts day by day. I know that his truth cannot lie: he has promised to reform her through much suffering on the part of his servants and by means of continual humble prayers made with tears and sweat.

Such a prayer is this.

63

PRAYER 8

To you, O heavenly doctor,[1]
my soul's boundless love,
I sigh mightily.
To you, O eternal infinite Trinity,
I the finite one cry out   5
within the mystic body of holy Church
for you to blot out by grace my soul's every stain.
And I cry out to you:
wait no longer,
but through the merits of this pilot of your ship—   10
St. Peter, I mean—
with the fire of charity
and the deep abyss of eternal wisdom
come to the aid of your bride
who is waiting for help.   15
Do not scorn your servants' desire
but even now,
O worker of peace,
guide this ship into the port of peace
and direct your servants toward yourself   20
so that the darkness may be lifted
and the dawn may appear—
the dawn which is the light
of those who have been planted in your Church
out of pure desire for the salvation of souls.[2]   25

Blessed,
O most generous Father,
be the chain you have given us
with which we can tie the hands of your justice,
the chain of your servants' humble faithful prayer   30
ablaze with desire,
for you have promised to use them
to be merciful to the world.[3]
I thank you,
O high eternal Godhead   35

because you have promised
to give your bride relief soon.
As for me,
I shall enter her garden once again
and never come out 40
until you fulfill your promises—
which have never been other than true.[4]

Cancel out our sins today, then,
O true God,
and wash our souls' face 45
with your only-begotten Son's blood,
poured out for us,
so that dead to ourselves
and living for him
we may offer him a return for his suffering[5] 50
with bright face
and undivided soul.[6]

So listen to us
as we pray for the guardian of this chair of yours,
whose feast we are celebrating. 55
Make your vicar
whatever sort of successor you would have him be
to your dear elder Peter,
and give him what is needed for your Church.
I am the witness 60
that you have promised to grant my desires soon;
with even more confidence then
I beg you to wait no longer
to fulfill these promises, O my God.

And you, 65
dearest children,
since we are committed,
it is time to work for Christ's Church,
the true mother of our faith.
So I urge you 70
who have already been planted in this Church
to be like pillars for her.

Let all of us together,
having cast off all selfish love and laziness,
work for that in this garden of saving faith   75
with the fervor of prayer
and with our deeds,
that we may perfectly fulfill the will of God eternal,
who has called us to this
for our own salvation   80
and that of others,
and for the unity of this Church[7]
in which is our souls' salvation.
Amen.

NOTES

1. Catherine often refers to God and to Christ as doctor. Cf. Mt. 9, 12 and Lk. 5, 31: "The healthy do not need a doctor; sick people do." (Cavallini)

2. The reference, as in Prayer 7, is to the newly appointed cardinals. Catherine saw the hope for Church reform in the appointment of spiritually motivated ministers to replace those who were corrupt and unworthy. (Cavallini)

3. Cf. *Dial.* 15, p. 54: "But I have one remedy to calm my wrath: my servants who care enough to press me with their tears and bind me with the chain of their desire. You see, you have bound me with that chain—and I myself gave you that chain because I wanted to be merciful to the world. I put into my servants a hunger and longing for my honor and the salvation of souls so that I might be forced by their tears to soften the fury of my divine justice."

4. Cf. Ps. 110, 4: "The Lord has sworn, and he will not repent." 2 Pt. 3, 9: "The Lord does not delay in keeping his promise." Was Catherine on this feast of the Chair of St. Peter perhaps thinking of that January 18 just two years earlier, when her great desire had been fulfilled in Pope Gregory XI's being at last "in his proper place" after his triumphal entry into Rome the night before? (Cavallini)

5. Cf. Gal. 2, 19: ". . . I died to the law to live for God." Phil. 3, 8–10: "For his sake I have forfeited everything; I have accounted all else rubbish so that Christ may be my wealth and I may be in him. . . . I wish to know Christ and the power flowing from his resurrection; likewise to know how to share in his sufferings by being formed into the pattern of his death."

6. A possible allusion to Mt. 6, 17–18: "When you fast, see to it that you groom your hair and wash your face . . . and your Father who sees what is hidden will repay you." (Cavallini)

7. Cf. Let. 327: "Nothing must keep you [from responding to Pope Urban's call]. . . . You must not say, 'I want my soul's peace; I can call out to God in

prayer.' No, for the love of Christ crucified! For now is not the time to be seeking yourself for your own sake, nor to be fleeing suffering in order to have consolations. No, it is time to be losing yourself. . . . So I beg and urge you in Christ gentle Jesus to come quickly to fulfill God's will. . . . Come to suffer, not to find pleasure, unless it be the pleasure of the cross. Look forward and get out onto the field to fight truly for the truth."

PRAYER 9

Sexagesima Sunday,[1] February 13, 1379.
At Rome.

Prayer 9 begins a series of seven recorded in almost daily succession from February 13, the second Sunday before Lent, through February 22, Shrove Tuesday. Those in the series for which the earliest rubrics give a year are dated 1378. However, the old Sienese calendar, according to which many of Catherine's prayers and letters are dated, began the new year on March 25, and was therefore a year behind the Roman calendar from January 1 to March 24 each year. Since Catherine was not in Rome during February and March of 1378, and the rubrics consistently place these prayers in Rome, the year must be read as 1379. (Besides, February 13 was a Sunday in 1379, but not in 1378.)

Giuliana Cavallini points out striking parallels between the first four of these prayers and Catherine's *Dialogue,* especially the sections of the latter entitled "The Bridge," "Tears," and "Truth." In both Catherine speaks of God's gifts to humanity and of the path to that human perfection which consists in union with God in love. In both she considers the path of spiritual progress from three perspectives: love, sorrow, and enlightenment. The sequence varies, but the basic themes are the same.

68

PRAYER 9

O immeasurable love!
O gentle love!
Eternal fire!
You are that fire ever blazing,[2]
O high eternal Trinity!   5
You are direct
without any twisting,
genuine
without any duplicity,
open   10
without any pretense.
Turn the eye of your mercy on your creatures.
I know that mercy is your hallmark,
and no matter where I turn
I find nothing but your mercy.[3]   15
This is why I run crying to your mercy
to have mercy on the world.

You want us to serve you
in your way,
eternal Father,   20
and you guide your servants in different ways
along different paths.
And so today you show us
that we neither may nor can in any way judge
what is within a person   25
by the actions we see.[4]
Rather we should judge all things according to your will—
and most of all where your servants are concerned
who are united with your will
and transformed in it.   30
This is why the soul is happy
when in your light she sees the light
of the endlessly different ways and paths
she sees in these servants of yours.[5]

For though they travel by different ways,   35
they are all running along the fiery road
of your charity;
otherwise they would not be following your truth
in truth.
So we see some of them running along the way of penance,   40
their foundation in physical mortification;
others have their foundation in humility,
in killing their selfish will;
others, in a lively faith;
others, in mercy;   45
and others, in letting go of themselves,
totally opened out in charity for their neighbors.[6]
By acting in such ways
the soul grows fat
who has conscientiously used the natural light[7]   50
and so attained that light beyond nature
by which she sees the boundless generosity
of your goodness.
Oh, how royally souls like this travel!
In everything   55
they see your will,
and so in everything your creatures do
they look for your will,
never passing judgment on the creature's intention.
O boundless charity!   60
Well have they learned
and kept in their heart
your Truth's teaching when he said,
"Do not judge according to appearances"![8]

O eternal Truth,   65
what is your teaching
and what is the way
by which you want us to go to the Father,
the way by which we must go?
I know of no other road   70
but the one you paved
with the true and solid virtues
of your charity's fire.
You, eternal Word,

cemented it with your blood,   *75*
so this must be the road.[9]
Our sin lies in nothing else
but in loving what you hate
and hating what you love.
I confess, eternal God,   *80*
that I have constantly loved what you hate
and hated what you love.
But today I cry out in the presence of your mercy:
grant that I may follow your truth
with a simple heart;   *85*
give me the deep well and fire of charity;
give me a continual hunger
to endure pains and torments for you.
Eternal Father,
give my eyes a fountain of tears[10]   *90*
with which to draw your mercy down
over all the world,
and especially over your bride.

O boundless, gentlest charity!
This is your garden,   *95*
implanted in your blood
and watered with that of your martyrs,
who ran bravely after the fragrance of your own.[11]
Do you, then, be the one to watch over it.
For who could prevail   *100*
over the city you were guarding?[12]
Set our hearts ablaze
and plunge them into this blood
so that we may more surely conceive a hunger
for your honor   *105*
and the salvation of souls.
I have sinned against the Lord.
I have sinned!
Have mercy on me!

O eternal Godhead!   *110*
What shall we say of you?
Or what judgment shall we make about you?

We shall judge and say
that you are our gentle God
who wants nothing other   *115*
than that we be made holy.[13]
This is unmistakably revealed to us
in the blood of your Son,
who for our salvation
ran as one in love   *120*
to the shameful death of the most holy cross.
We should be ashamed to lift our heads in pride
when we see you,
God most high,
brought down to the mud of our humanity.   *125*

O eternal Godhead,
how fitting mercy is to you![14]
It suits you so well
that your servants arouse your mercy
against the judgment the world deserves   *130*
because of its sins!
Your mercy created us,
and the same mercy redeemed us from eternal death.[15]
Your mercy rules over us
and holds back your justice,   *135*
keeping the earth from opening up to swallow us,
keeping the animals from devouring us.
In fact, all things serve us
and the earth gives us its fruits.[16]
All this your mercy does.   *140*
Your mercy preserves us
and prolongs our life,
giving us time to return and be reconciled with you.[17]

O compassionate merciful Father,
who keeps the angels from taking revenge   *145*
on this humanity which is your enemy?
Your mercy.
In mercy you grant us consolation to coax us to love,
for the creature's heart
is attracted by love.   *150*

The same mercy gives and permits sufferings and hardships
so that we may learn to know ourselves
and acquire the little virtue of true humility—
and even to give yourself a reason
to reward those who fight bravely,   *155*
suffering with true patience.
In mercy you preserved the scars in your Son's body
so that he might with these scars
beg for mercy for us before your majesty.[18]
In mercy you have seen fit today to show me,   *160*
poor as I am,
how we can in no way pass judgment
on other people's intentions.[19]
Indeed, by sending people along an endless variety of paths,
you give me an example for myself,   *165*
and for this I thank you.

Your mercy did not will
that the spotless Lamb should redeem the human race
with just a single drop of his blood,
nor with pain in just one part of his body,   *170*
but with his whole body's pain and blood.
Thus he would make complete atonement
for the whole human race
that had sinned against you.[20]
We see that some of your creatures sin against you   *175*
with their hands,
others with their feet,
others with their head,
others with other parts of their body—
so the human race had sinned against you   *180*
with every part of the body.
Besides,
since every sin is committed with the will,
without which there would be no sin,
and since this will embraces the whole body,   *185*
therefore the whole human body sins against you.
This is why you wanted to make atonement
with the whole of your Son's body and blood;
thus everything would be fully atoned for
by the power of the infinite divine nature   *190*

joined with finite human nature.
In the Word
our humanity endured the pain
and the Godhead accepted the sacrifice.[21]

O eternal Word,   *195*
Son of God,
how can it be that you had perfect contrition for sin
when the poison of sin was not in you?[22]
I see, boundless love,
that you wanted to make atonement   *200*
both physically and spiritually[23]
because we humans had sinned
both physically and spiritually.

I have sinned against the Lord.
Have mercy on me!   *205*
Do not look at our sins,
all-powerful, compassionate, merciful God!
Amen.

NOTES

1. In the former liturgical calendar, the three Sundays before Lent were designated as Septuagesima, Sexagesima, and Quinquagesima.

2. Cf. Mal. 3,2: "For he is like the refiner's fire." Heb. 12, 29: "For our God is a consuming fire" (Dt. 4,24). Is. 33, 14: "Who of us can live with the consuming fire? who of us can live with the everlasting flames?" In all of these texts, however, the allusion is to God only as purifying. Catherine's use of the fire image always stresses the role of warmth and light as well as that of purification.

3. Cf. *Dial.* 30, p. 72: "O mercy! My heart is engulfed with the thought of you! For wherever I turn my thoughts I find nothing but mercy!"

4. Cf. Jn. 7, 24: "Stop judging by appearances and make an honest judgment!" Is. 11, 3: "Not by appearance shall he judge, nor by hearsay shall he decide." Rom. 14, 10: "But you, how can you sit in judgment on your brother or sister?"

5. Cf. *Dial.* 100, p. 189: "They [i.e., souls who live in 'most perfect light'] find joy in everything. They do not sit in judgment on my servants or anyone else, but rejoice in every situation and every way of living they see, saying, 'Thanks to

you, eternal Father, that in your house there are so many dwelling places!' And they are happier to see many different ways than if they were to see everyone walking the same way, because this way they see the greatness of my goodness more fully revealed."

6. For a more expanded treatment, cf. *Dial.* 98–100, pp. 184ff., and Let. 64 and 65.

7. I.e., the power of understanding.

8. Jn. 7, 24.

9. In the *Dialogue* Catherine develops in great detail this image of the bridge. Cf. 27, p. 66: "This bridge has walls of stone so that travelers will not be hindered when it rains. Do you know what these stones are? They are the stones of true solid virtue. . . . [T]he Word, my gentle Son . . . built them into walls, tempering the mortar with his own blood. That is, his blood was mixed into the mortar of his divinity with the strong heat of burning love."

10. Cf. Jer. 8, 23: "Oh, that my head were a spring of water, my eyes a fountain of tears, that I might weep day and night over the slain of the daughter of my people!"

11. Cf. Sg. 1, 3–4: "Your name spoken is a spreading perfume—that is why maidens love you. Draw me! We will follow you eagerly!"

12. Cf. Is. 37, 35: "I will shield and save this city for my own sake. . . ." Ps. 127, 1: "Unless the Lord guard the city, in vain does the guard keep vigil."

13. 1 Thes. 4, 3: "It is God's will that you grow in holiness."

14. Cf. Ps. 62, 13: ". . . and yours, O Lord, is kindness."

15. *Dial.* 30, p. 71: "By your mercy we were created. And by your mercy we were created anew in your Son's blood. It is your mercy that preserves us. Your mercy made your Son play death against life and life against death on the wood of the cross. In him life confounded the death that is our sin, even while that same death of sin robbed the spotless Lamb of his bodily life."

16. Cf. *Dial.* 140, p. 288: "No, it was only my mercy. Constrained by my very self, I made the heavens and the earth, the sea and the vault of the sky to move above you, the air so that you might breathe, fire and water each to temper the other, and the sun so that you would not be left in darkness. All these I made and put in order to serve the needs of humankind. The sky adorned with birds, the earth bringing forth its fruits, the many animals all for the life of humankind, the sea adorned with fish—everything I made with the greatest order and providence."

17. Cf. *Dial.* 46, p. 95: "Sometimes I lend them time, or I put them into my servants' hearts and because of their constant prayers they escape from their sin and wretchedness."

18. Cf. Rom. 8, 34: "Who shall condemn them? Christ Jesus . . . who is at the right hand of God and who intercedes for us?" Heb. 7, 25: "Therefore he is always able to save those who approach God through him, since he forever lives to make intercession for them."

19. In the *Dialogue* (100–107, pp. 187ff.) God speaks to Catherine at length on the matter of judgment, after which (108, p. 202) she give thanks: "Thanks, thanks to you, eternal Father! . . . You gave me . . . a medicine against a hidden

sickness I had not recognized, by teaching me that I can never sit in judgment on any person. . . ."

20. Cf. *S.Th.* III, q. 46, a. 5.

21. *Dial.* 22, p. 59: "The earth of human nature by itself, as I have told you, was incapable of atoning for sin. . . . Your nature had to be joined with the height of mine, the eternal Godhead, before it could make atonement for all of humanity. Then human nature could endure the suffering, and the divine nature, joined with that humanity, would accept my Son's sacrifice on your behalf to release you from death and give you life." Also *S. Th.* III, q. 48, a. 6.

22. Cf. 1 Jn. 3, 5: ". . . in him there was nothing sinful." *Dial.* 26, p. 65: "So the bridge has three stairs, and you can reach the last by climbing the first two. The last stair is so high that the flooding waters cannot strike it—for the venom of sin never touched my Son."

23. Cf. *S. Th.* III, q. 46, a. 6r.

PRAYER 10

Monday, February 14, 1379.
At Rome.

The date of this prayer is provided by S1.

† † †

PRAYER 10

O eternal Trinity!
Eternal Trinity!
O fire and deep well of charity!
O you who are madly in love
with your creature!   5
O eternal truth!
O eternal fire!
O eternal wisdom
given for our redemption!
But did your wisdom come into the world alone?   10
No.
For wisdom was not separate from power,
nor was power without mercy.
You, wisdom, did not come alone then,
but the whole Trinity was there.[1]   15
O eternal Trinity,
mad with love,
of what use to you was our redemption?
None at all,
for you have no need of us,   20
you who are our God.
For whose good was it?
Only humanity's.

O boundless charity!
Just as you gave us yourself,   25
wholly God and wholly human,
so you left us all of yourself as food
so that while we are pilgrims in this life
we might not collapse in our weariness
but be strengthened by you, heavenly food.[2]   30
O mercenary people!
And what has your God left you?[3]
He has left you himself,
wholly God and wholly human,
hidden under the whiteness of this bread.   35

O fire of love!
Was it not enough to gift us
with creation in your image and likeness,
and to create us anew to grace in your Son's blood,
without giving us yourself as food,   40
the whole of divine being,
the whole of God?
What drove you?
Nothing but your charity,
mad with love as you are!   45

And just as you did not send the Word alone
as gift for our redemption,
so you left us not him alone as food,
but, as I have said, the whole divine being,
as one mad with love for your creature.[4]   50
Even more—
just as you did not leave us only yourself as food,
so you do not give only yourself
to the soul who turns her back on herself completely
for love of you   55
and desires and seeks
only the glory and praise of your name.
(Such a soul seeks you not for selfish reasons,
but because you are supreme eternal goodness
worthy of your creatures' love and service.   60
Nor does she love her neighbors for her own sake
but for yours,
to give you glory.)
To such as these you do not give just yourself.
No, you make them strong in your own power   65
against the devil's assaults,
against other people's abuse,
against the rebelliousness of their own flesh,
against all anguish and trouble
from whatever source it may come.   70
You enlighten them with your Son's wisdom
to know both themselves and your truth
as well as the devil's secret deceits.
And you set their hearts ablaze
with the Holy Spirit's fire,   75

with desire to love and follow you in truth.
All this you do in your servants
in proportion to the measure of love
with which each one comes to you,
and according to the way   80
each has used your gift of natural light.[5]

Thanks,
thanks to you,
most high eternal Father,
for showing us today—   85
madly in love as you are with your creature—
how your bride, holy Church,
can be reformed.[6]
And I beg you,
since you have on the one hand provided   90
by enlightening our mind's eye regarding this need,
so now on the other hand provide
by disposing your ministers,
and most especially your vicar,
to follow the light you have poured forth   95
and will yet pour forth.

O eternal Trinity,
I have sinned all my life long!
O my wretched soul,
have you ever given a thought to your God?   100
Surely not,
for if you had,
you would be ablaze
in the furnace of his charity.[7]

Eternal God,   105
restore health to the sick
and life to the dead.
Give us a voice,
your own voice,
to cry out to you   110
for mercy for the world

and for the reform of holy Church.
And listen to your own voice
with which we cry to you.[8]
And while I cry out to you in general for the whole world,   *115*
I cry out to you most particularly
for your vicar and for his pillars,[9]
as well as for all those you have given me
to love with a special love.
Even though I am sick,   *120*
I want to see them healthy;
and even though I am less than perfect
because of my sins,
I want to see them perfect;
and even though I am dead,   *125*
I want to see them alive in your grace.[10]

O immense fire and affection of charity!
What is the source of such humility and mercy
that you, God, shared so much with your human creature—
by joining your divine nature with human nature,   *130*
as well as by the new creation you have granted us
in your image and likeness,
and by the sense of union with you
that you give the soul who loves and serves you
with a sincere and generous heart?[11]   *135*
It does not come from our goodness,
for we are devils incarnate,
enemies to you.
No,
it comes only from the fire of your charity.   *140*
How ashamed we should be
for not making our constant dwelling place in you[12]
with all our heart,
even though you,
high eternal Trinity,   *145*
make your dwelling place with us
in so many ways!
O my wretched soul!
It is because you have never given a thought to your God
that you have not grounded your heart firmly   *150*
in true virtue.

I have sinned against the Lord.
Have mercy on me!

You, eternal Godhead,
are life   *155*
and I am death.
You are wisdom
and I am ignorance.
You are light
and I am darkness.   *160*
You are infinite
and I am finite.
You are absolute directness
and I am terrible twistedness.
You are the doctor   *165*
and I am sick.
And who could ever reach up to you,
supreme exaltedness,
eternal Godhead,
to thank you for such infinite blessings   *170*
as you have given us?
You yourself will reach up to you[13]
with the light you will pour out
into all who are willing to receive it,
and with your own cord   *175*
you will bind all who will let themselves be bound
by not resisting your will.

Do not be slow,
most kind Father,
to turn the eye of your mercy on the world.   *180*
Even though you draw glory and praise for your name
from everything,
you will be more glorified by giving people light
than by their remaining in the dark and blindness
of deadly sin.[14]   *185*
So we see your glory shining forth
in sinners
because of the mercy you show them
by not drawing the sword of your justice against them[15]

and by even lending them time   190
so they may turn back to you.
And in hell
your glory shines forth
in the justice paid to the damned—
though you are merciful even to them,   195
since they do not suffer as much as they deserve—
and this mercy and justice
reflect glory and praise to your name.
But I want to see
the glory and praise of your name   200
in your creatures' following your will
and so reaching the goal for which you created them.[16]
And I want you to make your vicar
to be another yourself—
because he has much greater need   205
of perfect light
than others do,
since he must be able
to give everyone else light.[17]

Grant us,   210
most kind and compassionate Father,
your gentle and eternal benediction.
Amen.

NOTES

1. Cf. *S. Th.* III, q. 3, a. 4r.

2. A probable allusion to the forty-day journey of the prophet Elijah, for which he was fortified by food which he ate at an angel's orders (1 Kg. 19, 5–8), as well as to Jesus' words before the miraculous feeding of the crowd: "My heart is moved with pity for the crowd. By now they have been with me three days. . . . I do not wish to send them away hungry, for fear they may collapse on the way." (Mt. 15, 32) (Cavallini)

3. The image of human greed for selfish and petty things appears in all its meanness in contrast with God's generosity. Cf. *Dial.* 30, p. 72: "O mad lover! It was not enough for you to take on our humanity: you had to die as well! Nor was death enough. . . . I see your mercy pressing you to give us even more when you leave yourself to us as food to strengthen our weakness, so that we forgetful fools should be forever reminded of your goodness." (Cavallini)

4. Cf. *Dial.* 110, p. 206: "His most gracious blood is a sun, wholly God and wholly human, for he is one thing with me and I with him. My power is not separate from his wisdom; nor is the heat, the fire of the Holy Spirit, separate from me the Father or from him the Son, for the Holy Spirit proceeds from me the Father and from him the Son, and we are one and the same Sun."

5. Both the worth of our actions (cf. *Dial.* 165, p. 357) and the fruit we receive from the Eucharist are in proportion to our love. In *Dial.* 110, p. 207f., Catherine illustrates the latter at length with the image of candles whose capacity for light varies according to their size. (Cavallini)

6. Catherine does not here elaborate on the "how"—though she does at length in the *Dialogue,* 110–134, p. 205ff. The wording here, however, suggests that Catherine might possibly have picked up the theme of reform from the day's liturgy.

7. Knowledge of God not translated into love is inconceivable for Catherine. The "gentle first Truth" revealed to us in the Incarnation is the "Word breathing forth love"; cf. *St. Th.* I, q. 43, a. 6 ad 2^m. (Cavallini)

8. God's own voice with which we cry out to him is the blood of Christ, "which speaks more eloquently than that of Abel." (Heb. 12, 24) Cf. also *Dial.* 134, p. 276: "His blood is ours because you have made of it a bath for us, and you neither can nor will refuse it to those who ask it of you in truth. Give then the fruit of the blood to these creatures of yours." (Cavallini)

9. Catherine calls "pillars" those who are meant to be a support to the Pope and the Church, probably here the cardinals. In *Dial.* 108, p. 203, she refers to her own spiritual directors as her "pillars." (Cavallini)

10. Cf. 2 Cor. 13, 9: "We even rejoice when we are weak and you are strong. Our prayer is that you may be built up to completion."

11. Cf. *Dial.* 78, p. 145ff., for a fuller treatment of the perfect soul's sense of God's presence.

12. Cf. Jn. 14, 23: "Those who love me will be true to my word, and my Father will love them; we will come to them and make our dwelling place with them."

13. Cf. *Dial.* 134, p. 273: "Can I, wretch that I am, repay the graces and burning charity you have shown . . . ? No, only you, most gentle loving Father, only you can be my acknowledgment and my thanks. The affection of your very own charity will offer you thanks, for I am she who is not." Heb. 13, 15: "Through him let us continually offer God a sacrifice of praise, that is, the fruit of lips which acknowledge his name."

14. Cf. Jn. 15, 8: "My Father has been glorified in your bearing much fruit and becoming my disciples." *Dial.* 134, p. 276: "For it would seem you would receive more glory and praise by saving so many people than by letting them stubbornly persist in their hardness."

15. Cf. Ez. 21, 8–10: "Thus says the Lord: See! I am coming at you; I will draw my sword from its sheath and cut off from you the virtuous and the wicked. . . . I, the Lord, have drawn my sword from its sheath, and it shall not be sheathed again."

16. Cf. *Dial.* 13, p. 49: "My Lord, turn the eye of your mercy on your people. . . . How much greater would be your glory if you would pardon so many and give them the light of knowledge . . . than to have praise only from my wretched self. . .! It is my will, then, and I beg it as a favor, that you have mercy on your people with the same eternal love that led you to create us in your image and likeness. . . . And this you did, eternal Trinity, willing that we should share all that you are, high eternal Trinity!"

17. Cf. Prayer 1: "Open the eye of your vicar on earth . . . because we receive our example for living from the good shepherd."

PRAYER 11

Tuesday, February 15, 1379.
At Rome.[1]

Once again Catherine's prayer seems to be inspired by what she has heard in the day's liturgy: "Today your Truth, with wonderful light, points out the source of darkness, that stinking garment, the selfish will. And your Truth reveals as well the means by which we come to know the light, the garment of your gentle will." The entire prayer is a development of these interwoven themes of darkness and light, clothing and dispossessing, self-will and God's will. No one biblical passage clearly suggests itself as the source of Catherine's thoughts, and here as in a number of other prayers our understanding would be greatly helped by a knowledge of the liturgical readings in which the saint was actually immersed day by day. Perhaps, too, there was the influence of a homily which had pulled together for her threads from all the readings for that day, the Tuesday after Sexagesima.

PRAYER 11

Eternal Godhead!
O high eternal Godhead!
Boundless love!
In your light I have seen light;
in your light I have come to know the light.[2]   5
in your light
we come to know the source of light
and the source of darkness—
that you are the source of all light,
and we the source of darkness.[3]   10
In your light
we come to know what light does in the soul,
and what darkness does.[4]
Your works are wonderful,[5] eternal Trinity!
In your light they are known   15
because they come forth from you who are light.

Today your Truth, with wonderful light,
points out the source of darkness,
that stinking garment,
the selfish will.   20
And your Truth reveals as well
the means by which we come to know the light,
the garment of your gentle will.
What a marvelous thing,
that even while we are in the dark   25
we should know the light!
that in finite things
we should know the infinite!
that even while we exist in death
we should know life![6]   30
Your Truth shows us
that the soul must strip herself of her selfish will
if she wants to be clothed perfectly in yours,
just as one turns one's garment inside out
when one undresses.[7]   35

And how do we so strip ourselves?
By the light which we receive
when with the hand of free choice
we use the light we received in holy baptism—
for in the light we have seen light.   40
And from what source does the soul receive this light?
Only from you who are light—
and you have revealed this light to us
under the veil of our own humanity.
And what does the soul receive   45
who has been clothed in this light?
She is relieved of darkness
and hunger
and thirst
and death.   50
For hunger for virtue
drives out hunger for her selfish will;
thirst for your honor
drives out thirst for her own honor;
and the life of your grace   55
has driven out the death of sin
and of her own disordered will.[8]

O stinking garment of our own will!
You do not clothe the soul;
you unclothe it!   60
O dispossessed will,
earnest of eternal life!
You are faithful even to the point of death—
faithful not to the world
but to your most gentle Creator.   65
And you bind the soul to him
because she has been completely freed
from herself.

What will tell the soul
that she is perfectly freed from herself?   70
Her no longer seeking
to have the time and the place in her own way
but in yours.

This is the lightsome garment.
It is indeed a sun, 75
for just as the sun shines on the earth
and warms it
and makes it bear fruit,[9]
so this true light warms the soul who possesses it
within the fire of your charity. 80
And it shines on her,
for with its light
it lets her know the truth
in the light of your wisdom.
And it makes her bear fruit 85
while she is in this mortal life—
the fruit of true solid virtue.

What keeps a soul from so dispossessing herself?
Her not having light
because she has neither recognized nor used 90
the basic light
you have given to every rational creature.[10]
Why has she not recognized it?
Because she has darkened her mind's eye with sin,
and with this same sin she has bound her will, 95
the will that is responsible for every sin.[11]
O my foolish soul!
How is it you fail to smell
the stench of sin?
How is it you are insensitive to 100
the fragrance of grace and virtue?
Because you have no light!
I have sinned against the Lord;
have mercy on me!

O God eternal, 105
in your light I have seen
how closely you have conformed your creature
to yourself.
I see that you have set us, as it were,
in a circle, 110
so that wherever we may go
we are still within this circle.[12]

If I set myself to know in your light
the being you have given us,
I see that you have granted us the gift   *115*
of fashioning us after your own image and likeness,[13]
sharing yourself,
eternal Trinity,
in the soul's three powers.
If I consider the Word,   *120*
through whom we are created anew to grace,
I see you fashioned after us
and us after you
through the union that you, eternal God,
have effected with humankind.[14]   *125*
And if I turn to the soul
enlightened by you, true light,
I see her making her continual dwelling place in you
by following your Truth's teaching,[15]
generally as well as particularly—   *130*
I mean in particular virtues,
proved by the love
that the soul has conceived in your light.
And you are love itself.
So the soul who follows your Truth's teaching   *135*
in love
becomes through love
another you.
Dispossessed of her own will,
she is so well clothed in yours   *140*
that she neither seeks nor desires anything
but what you seek and will for her.[16]

You are in love with such a soul,
and she with you.
But you love her gratuitously,   *145*
since you loved her before she came to be,[17]
while she loves you
because it is her duty.
She has come to know
that she cannot love you gratuitously,   *150*
since it is she who is obligated to you,
not you to her,

and she has seen that this free love
which she cannot give to you
she must give to her neighbors,   155
loving them gratuitously
and at the same time because it is her duty.[18]
She loves them gratuitously
because she does not look for a return from them,
nor does she serve them   160
for any profit she might get from them
but only for love;
and she loves them out of duty
because you command it
and it is her duty to obey you.[19]   165

I reflect
how conformed with yourself you make the soul
when she rises up by the light of understanding
received from you, true light,
and gazes upon herself   170
in the light of your truth
with her affection set on you.
And then I see
that you who are God immortal
allow her to know the good things   175
that are immortal,
and you let her enjoy them
in your charity's affection.
You who are light
allow her to share in the light   180
with you.
You who are fire
share the fire with her,
and in the fire
you fuse your will with hers   185
and hers with yours.
You, wisdom,
give her wisdom
to discern and recognize your truth.
You who are strength   190
give her strength,
and she becomes so strong

that neither demon nor any other creature
can deprive her of your strength
unless she herself wills it—   *195*
nor will she ever will it
so long as she wears the garment of your will,
for it is only her own will
by itself
that makes her weaken.   *200*
You who are infinite
make her infinite
by reason of the conformity you have brought about
between yourself and her—
by grace while she is a pilgrim in this life,[20]   *205*
and in everlasting life by her seeing you eternally.
There she becomes so perfectly conformed with you
that her free choice is enchained,
so that she can no longer be separated from you.[21]

Well do I proclaim, then,   *210*
that your Truth is speaking the truth,
that by grace
the creature is conformed with you in everything,
and you with her.
You give her not just a bit of grace   *215*
but all of it.
Why do I say all of it?
Because she lacks nothing for her salvation.[22]
True,
she is more or less perfect   *220*
in proportion as she is willing, in your light,
to put to use the natural light you have given her.[23]

What more shall I say?
Nothing,
except that you, God, became human   *225*
and humanity became God.
What was the cause of such a conformity?
The light,
in which humanity came to know your will.
Once we come to know it,   *230*

we dispossess ourselves of our own will—
which is darkness and nakedness and death to us—
and are clothed in yours,
clothed in you,
in grace,   235
in light,
in fire,
and in union.
So it is you
who are the cause of all good,   240
and it is our own disordered will
that is the cause of all evil
because it is clothed in selfish love.
It is the cause of so much evil
that it uses darkness   245
to make us stumble outside the circle
which is the light of most holy faith,
the circle within which we find you
no matter where we turn.
And what sort of conformity do we find,   250
and with what do we find ourselves joined,
once we have left the light?
We find ourselves rightly conformed with the beasts,
wholly irrational,
following the perverse law and teaching   255
of demons both visible and invisible.[24]

I confess, eternal God,
high eternal God,
and I do not deny it:
I am that wretched cause of all evil,   260
because I have not
in your light
put the light to use
so as to recognize how disgusting to you
and how hurtful to me   265
is the wicked stinking garment
of my disordered selfish will.
Nor have I recognized your gentle will,
in which I ought—
because it is my duty—   270

to clothe myself.
I have sinned.
I have sinned against the Lord.
Have mercy on me!

You, eternal God,   275
high eternal God—
in your light you make us see light.[25]
I humbly beg you, then:
pour out this light on everyone,
but especially on our dear father, your vicar—   280
as much as you must
to make of him
another you.
And give light to those who are in darkness,
so that in your light   285
they may come to know and love the truth.[26]
I pray to you, too,
for all those you have given me
to love with a special love,
with special concern.   290
Let them be illumined with your light.
Let all imperfection be taken from them,
so that in truth
they may work in your garden,[27]
where you have assigned them to work.   295
Punish and avenge their sins and imperfections
in me,
for I am the cause of them.
I have sinned against the Lord.
Have mercy on me!   300

Thanks,
thanks to you,
high eternal Trinity,
for in your light you have refreshed my soul
by letting me see how we,   305
your creatures,
are conformed with you,
and by teaching me how surpassing wonderful is your will.

I am the one who is not,
and you are the one who is.[28]   *310*
Do you yourself then
offer yourself thanks
by giving me the ability to praise you.[29]
Let your will urge you
to be merciful to the world,   *315*
and to come with your divine help
to the aid of your vicar
and your sweet bride.

I have sinned against the Lord.
Have mercy on me!   *320*

High eternal Godhead,
grant us your gentle benediction.
Amen.

NOTES

1. S1 supplies the date and place.

2. Cf. Ps. 36, 10: "For with you is the fountain of life, and in your light we see light."

3. Cf. Jn. 3, 19: ". . . the light came into the world, but people loved darkness rather than light because their deeds were wicked."

4. Cf. Jn. 3, 20–21: "All who practice evil hate the light, they do not come near it for fear their deeds will be exposed. But those who act in truth come into the light, to make it clear that their deeds are done in God."

5. Cf. Rv. 15, 3: "Mighty and wonderful are your works, Lord God almighty!" Also Ps. 92, 6; 104, 24; 139, 14.

6. Catherine has a vivid sense of opposites and of the positive value of paradox: virtues are not achieved except "through their opposites" and "one should not be sad or run away in times of darkness, for out of the darkness the light is born." (Let. 211, LXX) Cf. also Jn. 1, 5: "The light shines on in darkness. . . ." (Cavallini)

7. Eph. 4, 22–24: ". . . you must lay aside your former way of life and the old self which deteriorates through illusion and desire, and acquire a fresh, spiritual way of thinking. You must put on that new person created in God's image, whose justice and holiness are born of truth." Rv. 3, 17–18: "You keep saying, 'I am so rich and secure that I want for nothing.' Little do you realize how wretch-

ed you are, how pitiable and poor, how blind and naked! Take my advice. . . . Buy white garments in which to be clothed, if the shame of your nakedness is to be covered." Mt. 16, 24: "If you wish to come after me, you must deny your very self, take up your cross, and begin to follow in my footsteps."

8. This new list of opposites casts light on the metaphor of the two garments, as well as the reference above (11. 31–35) to turning inside out the garment of one's selfish will. (Cavallini)

9. Cf. Is. 61, 10–11: "I rejoice heartily in the Lord, in my God is the joy of my soul; for he has clothed me with a robe of salvation, and wrapped me in a mantle of justice. . . . As the earth brings forth its plants, and a garden makes its growth spring up, so will the Lord God make justice and praise spring up before all the nations."

10. Cf. *Dial.* 98, p. 184f: "You know that no one can walk in the way of truth without the light of reason that you draw from me, the true Light, through the eye of your understanding. You must have as well the light of faith, which you possess as my gift from holy baptism—unless you have put it out with your sins."

11. Cf. *Dial.* 43, p. 88: "But if you refuse to put this weapon, your will, into the devil's hands (that is, if you refuse to consent to his tempting and troubling) you will never be hurt in any temptation by the guilt of sin."

12. *Dial.* 10, p. 41: "So think of the soul as a tree made for love and living only by love. . . . The circle in which this tree's root, the soul's love, must grow is true knowledge of herself, knowledge that is joined to me, who like the circle have neither beginning nor end. You can go round and round within this circle, finding neither end nor beginning, yet never leaving the circle."

13. Gn. 1, 26.

14. Cf. Rom. 8, 29: "Those whom he foreknew he predestined to share the image of his Son. . . ." 2 Cor. 5, 17: "This means that if anyone is in Christ, that person is a new creation."

15. Cf. Jn. 15, 10: "You will live in my love if you keep my commandments, even as I have kept my Father's commandments, and live in his love."

16. Cf. *Dial.* 100, p. 189: "Souls such as these have let go of themselves, have stripped off their old nature, their selfish sensuality, and clothed themselves in a new nature, the gentle Christ Jesus, my Truth, and they follow him courageously."

17. Cf. 1 Jn. 4, 10: "Love, then, consists in this: not that we have loved God but that he has loved us."

18. Cf. 1 Jn. 4, 11–12: "Beloved, if God has loved us so, we must have the same love for one another. . . . If we love one another God dwells in us, and his love is brought to perfection in us." Rom. 13, 8: "Owe no debt to anyone except the debt that binds us to love one another."

19. Mt. 22, 39; Rom. 13, 9.

20. Cf. *Dial.* 79, p. 147f: "For once souls have risen up in eager longing, they run in virtue along the bridge of the teaching of Christ crucified and . . . they taste in me the eternal Godhead, and I am to them a peaceful sea with

which the soul becomes so united that her spirit knows no movement but in me. Though she is mortal she tastes the reward of the immortals."

21. Cf. *Dial.* 41, p. 84: "So you see that in whatever bond of love they finish their lives, that bond is theirs forever and lasts eternally. They are so conformed to my will that they can will only what I will. When time came to an end for them and they died in grace, their freedom was so bound with the chains of charity that they are no longer capable of sin."

22. Cf. 1 Cor. 1, 4–7: "I continually thank my God for you because of the favor he has bestowed on you in Christ Jesus . . . that you lack no spiritual gift as you wait for the revelation of our Lord Jesus Christ."

23. Cf. *Dial.* 99, p. 186: "But once the soul has gained this ordinary light she ought not rest content. For as long as you are pilgrims in this life you are capable of growing and should grow. Those who are not growing are by that very fact going backward. Either you should be growing in that ordinary light that you have gained with the help of my grace, or you should be making a genuine effort to advance to the second and more perfect light, to rise from the imperfect to the perfect." Cf. also the parable of the "talents": Mt. 25, 14–30; Lk. 19, 12–26.

24. Cf. Mt. 22, 11–13: "When the king came in to meet the guests, however, he caught sight of a man not properly dressed for a wedding feast. . . . The king then said to the attendants, 'Bind him hand and foot and throw him out into the night. . . .' "

25. Cf. Ps. 36, 10: "For with you is the fountain of life, and in your light we see light." Also 1 Pt. 2, 9: ". . . the One who called you from darkness into his marvelous light."

26. Cf. Lk. 1, 78–79: "He, the Dayspring, shall visit us in his mercy to shine on those who sit in darkness and in the shadow of death." Mt. 4, 16: "A people living in darkness has seen a great light. On those who inhabit a land overshadowed by death, light has arisen."

27. I.e., the Church. Cf. *Dial.* 23–24, pp. 60–63.

28. Cf. *Life* X, p. 85: "Do you know, daughter, who you are and who I am? If you know these two things you have beatitude in your grasp. You are she who is not, and I AM HE WHO IS."

29. Cf. Ps. 71, 8: "My mouth shall be filled with your praise, with your glory day by day."

PRAYER 12

Wednesday, February 16, 1379.
At Rome.[1]

Catherine seems here almost to continue her prayer of the day before, picking up as she does a number of the same themes. Here, however, the theme of sin and ingratitude appears as a sort of counterpoint to the praise of God's gifts to humanity. And the image of God as fire is a motif throughout.

The prayer is remarkably similar to the beginning of Catherine's hymn to God as light and fire in the *Dialogue* (134, p. 273f.). In the larger Latin collections it is the twenty-second and final prayer, and Giuliana Cavallini compares its loftiness to that of the closing hymn of Catherine's book. Here as there she ends with the plea so central to her life, "to perfectly know and follow your Truth in truth, with a free and simple heart."

PRAYER 12

Eternal Godhead,
O high eternal Godhead!
O supreme eternal Father!
O fire ever blazing!
You, eternal Father,   5
high eternal Trinity,
you are the measureless fire of charity.
O Godhead, Godhead!
What is it that reveals your greatness and goodness?
The gift you gave to humankind.   10
And what did you give us?
Your whole self,
God,
eternal Trinity.[2]
Where were you given to us?   15
In the stable of our humanity,
which had truly become a stable,
a place for animals—
that is, for deadly sins—
to show us how far our humanity had sunk   20
because of sin.[3]
So you gave us your whole self,
God,
conforming yourself with our humanity.

O God eternal!   25
O God eternal!
You tell me to gaze into you,
high eternal Godhead,
and you want me
when I gaze into you,   30
to come to know myself,
so that in your exaltedness
I may better realize my baseness,
and your greatness
in my own smallness.   35

But I see that until I strip myself of myself,
of my disordered selfish will,
I cannot see you.
Therefore you have taught me
first to strip myself of my own will   40
by coming to know myself.
In that knowledge I find and come to know you,
and in coming to know you
my soul is more perfectly stripped of myself
and clothed in your will.   45
You want me, then,
to rise up in the light
to come to know myself in you.

O fire ever blazing!
The soul who comes to know herself in you   50
finds your greatness wherever she turns,
even in the tiniest things,
in people
and in all created things,
for in all of them she sees   55
your power
and wisdom
and mercy.[4]
For if you had not been powerful,
knowing,   60
and willing,
you would not have created them.
But you were powerful and knowing and willing,
and therefore you created everything.
O my poor blind soul,   65
you have never come to know yourself in him
because you have not stripped yourself
of your disordered will,
and have not clothed yourself
in his will.   70

And how, gentlest love,
do you want me to contemplate myself in you?
You want me to contemplate your gift to me—

your gift of creation
in your image and likeness. 75
In that creation,
supreme eternal purity,
you joined yourself with the mire of our humanity.
You were driven
by the fire of your charity, 80
and with that same fire
you left us yourself as food.
And what food is this?
Food of the angels,
supreme eternal purity! 85
This is why you want and demand such purity
of the soul who receives this most sweet sacrament—
such purity
that if it were possible for the angelic nature
to be purified 90
(a nature that has no need for purification),
such a great mystery
would demand that it be purified.[5]
And how shall the soul be purified?
In the fire of your charity 95
and by washing her face
in the blood of your only-begotten Son.
O my wretched soul!
How dare you approach such a great mystery
without purification? 100
Blush for shame,
you who deserve to live with beasts and devils
because you have always acted like a beast
and followed the devil's will!

Eternal goodness, 105
you want me to gaze into you
and see that you love me,
to see that you love me gratuitously,
so that I may love everyone
with the very same love. 110
You want me, then,
to love and serve my neighbors gratuitously,
by helping them

spiritually and materially
as much as I can,   *115*
without any expectation of selfish profit or pleasure.
Nor do you want me to hold back
because of their ingratitude or persecution,
or for any abuse I may suffer from them.
What then shall I do   *120*
to come to such a vision?
I shall strip myself
of my stinking garment,
and by the light of most holy faith
I shall contemplate myself in you.   *125*
And I shall clothe myself in your eternal will,
and by this light I shall come to know
that you, eternal Trinity,
are table
and food   *130*
and waiter for us.
You, eternal Father,
are the table
that offers us as food
the Lamb, your only-begotten Son.   *135*
He is the most exquisite of foods for us,
both in his teaching,
which nourishes us in your will,[6]
and in the sacrament
that we receive in holy communion,   *140*
which feeds and strengthens us
while we are pilgrim travelers in this life.
And the Holy Spirit
is indeed a waiter for us,
for he serves us this teaching   *145*
by enlightening our mind's eye with it
and inspiring us to follow it.[7]
And he serves us charity for our neighbors
and hunger to have as our food
souls   *150*
and the salvation of the whole world
for the Father's honor.[8]
So we see that souls enlightened in you,
true light,
never let a moment pass   *155*

without eating this exquisite food
for your honor.[9]

Love immeasurable,
in yourself you show us the world's need,
and even more the Church's need,   160
and the love you have for the Church
because she is founded in your Son's blood
and in her that blood is preserved.
You show us, too,
the love you have for your vicar,   165
because you have made him the minister of this blood.[10]
So I shall contemplate myself in you
so that I may become pure,
and thus purified
I shall cry out in the presence of your mercy   170
so that you may turn the eye of your compassion
toward the need of your bride,
and enlighten and strengthen your vicar.
Enlighten also, most perfectly,
your servants,   175
so that they may counsel him rightly and sincerely.
And make him willing
to follow the light you pour into them.[11]

You, high eternal wisdom,
did not leave the soul alone   180
but gave her the company of her three powers,
memory, understanding, and will.
These are so united among themselves
that whatever the one wants,
the others follow.   185
Thus, if memory sets itself
to consider your blessings and your boundless goodness,
the mind at once wants to understand them
and the will wants to love and follow your will.[12]
And because you did not leave the soul alone,   190
you do not want her to be alone,
without love for you
and affection for her neighbors.[13]

When she is in such company
she is perfectly united—   *195*
made one with you
and one with her neighbors
in the union of love and charity's affection.
So one can say as Paul said,
"Many run the race,   *200*
but one is the winner"—[14]
charity.
But when the soul takes sin as her companion
she stands alone
because she has left you   *205*
who are all good.
Once cut off from you
she is cut off from charity for her neighbors.
Sin is her companion,
and sin is nothingness.   *210*
Thus you show, eternal Truth,
how she stands alone.[15]
I have sinned against the Lord.
Have mercy on me!
Never have I come to know myself in you.   *215*
But it is your light
that allows us to see whatever good there is to know.[16]

In your nature,
eternal Godhead,
I shall come to know my nature.   *220*
And what is my nature, boundless love?
It is fire,
because you are nothing but a fire of love.
And you have given humankind
a share in this nature,   *225*
for by the fire of love
you created us.[17]
And so with all other people
and every created thing:
you made them out of love.   *230*
O ungrateful people!
What nature has your God given you?
His very own nature!

Are you not ashamed
to cut yourselves off from such a noble thing   235
through the guilt of deadly sin?

O eternal Trinity,
my sweet love!
You, light,
give us light.   240
You, wisdom,
give us wisdom.
You, supreme strength,
strengthen us.
Today, eternal God,   245
let our cloud be dissipated[18]
so that we may perfectly know and follow your Truth
in truth,
with a free and simple heart.

God, come to our assistance!   250
Lord, make haste to help us![19]
Amen.

NOTES

1. The year and place are supplied by R. The earliest extant reference to
the day, however, is found in the Latin edition of Birkmann, Coloniae Agrip-
pinae, 1601.

2. Cf. Jn. 4, 10: "If you only recognized God's gift. . . ."

3. In the *Dialogue* (151, p. 320) the stable is a symbol not of humanity's
degradation but of the potential for rebirth: "You see this gentle loving Word
born in a stable while Mary was on a journey, to show you pilgrims how you
should be constantly born anew in the stable of self-knowledge, where by grace
you will find me born within your soul." But, as becomes clear in the next lines,
it is precisely in coming to know our sinfulness in contrast with God's goodness
that we are able to be reborn.

4. Cf. *S. Th.* I, q. 45, a. 6.

5. Cf. *Dial.* 124, p. 237: ". . . were it possible for the angels to be purified, they would have to be purified for this mystery. But this is not possible; they
do not need to be purified, for the poison of sin cannot infect them."

6. Cf. Jn. 4, 34: "Doing the will of him who sent me and bringing his work to completion is my food."

7. Cf. Jn. 14, 26: ". . . the Holy Spirit, whom the Father will send in my name, will instruct you in everything, and remind you of all that I told you."

8. Cf. *Dial.* 78, p. 145f., for further reflections on the image of the Trinity as table, food, and waiter.

9. Cf. *Dial.* 100, p. 187ff.

10. Cf. *Dial.* 115, p. 215: "Christ on earth, then, has the keys to the blood."

11. One of Catherine's dreams was that Pope Urban VI should have a "council of the servants of God," in addition to his cardinals and political advisors, for, as she wrote to him (Let. 302), "When it comes to authority you can do everything, but when it comes to vision, you have only the insight of a single individual." Letters were, in fact, sent in December by both Urban and Catherine asking certain persons to meet in Rome on the second Sunday after Epiphany for this purpose, but the dream in the end met with little response and less effect.

12. Cf. *Dial.* 51–55, pp. 103–110.

13. Cf. *Dial.* 54, p. 102f.: ". . . you must gather together, as he said, either two or three or more. . . . One alone is excluded from my companionship, since I cannot be 'in the midst' of someone who has no companion. Those who are wrapped up in selfish love of themselves are alone, mere nothings, because they are cut off from my grace and from charity for their neighbors. . . . You know that all the commandments of the Law are comprised in two—to love me above all things and to love your neighbor as your very self—and without these two none of the commandments can be kept. . . . These two cannot be gathered together in my name without three—that is, without the gathering of the three powers of the soul: memory, understanding, and will. . . . When these three powers of the soul are gathered together, I am in their midst by grace."

14. 1 Cor. 9, 24.

15. Cf. *Dial.* 54, p. 107: "And once deprived of me through their own fault, they turn to nothingness—for I alone am who I am."

16. Cf. *Dial.* 167, p. 364: "For all these and so many other endless evils and sins of mine, your wisdom, your kindness, your mercy, your infinite goodness have not despised me. No, in your light you have given me light."

17. Cf. *S. Th.* I, q. 45, a. 6.

18. Cf. Let. 350: "What cuts us off from this true and gentle light? Selfish love, which is like a cloud that darkens the mind's eye and covers over the pupil which is the light of most holy faith."

19. This introductory invocation from the Liturgy of the Hours was particularly dear to Catherine. Cf. *Life* I, xi, p. 105: "It remained a favourite with her for the rest of her life. . . . She translated it into the vernacular, and would repeat it again and again."

PRAYER 13

Friday, February 18, 1379.
At Rome.

R places this prayer on February 19. A specifies Friday, on the basis of which G corrects the date to February 18, which fell on Friday in 1379.

Catherine's remembrance of the priest who had given her communion indicates that this prayer, as probably many of the others in the collection, was prayed just after the morning's Mass. The theme of communion recurs several times, with connotations deeply significant to Catherine. Communion for her is far more than a momentary personal tryst with Jesus, for Jesus embodies the total mystery—the sacrament—of God's truth and redeeming love, and to commune with him, in the Eucharist or in any other way, is to commune with the whole of that mystery. This is the mystery so vividly symbolized for Catherine in the blood: re-creation beyond the first gift of creation. In this mystery all mysteries, all sacraments, coalesce, and so a prayer that might seem at a casual reading to be disconnected and rambling is, in fact, very profoundly unified.

PRAYER 13

O high eternal Trinity,
boundless love!
And if you call me daughter,
I in turn
call you most high eternal Father.   *5*
And just as you give me yourself
by communicating to me
the body and blood of your only-begotten Son,
therein giving me all of God
and all of humanity,   *10*
so, boundless love,
I ask you to communicate to me
the mystic body of holy Church
and the universal body of Christianity.[1]
For in the fire of your charity   *15*
I have come to know that this is the food
in which you want the soul to delight.

You, eternal God,
saw me and knew me
in yourself.[2]   *20*
And because you saw me in your light
you fell in love with your creature
and drew her out of yourself
and created her in your image and likeness.[3]
But this did not make it possible   *25*
for me your creature
to know you in myself
except as I saw in myself
your image and likeness.
The lowliness of my understanding   *30*
could neither behold nor comprehend
your exaltedness.
Therefore,
so that I might see and know you in myself
and thus have perfect knowledge of you,   *35*

you made yourself one with us
by descending from your Godhead's great exaltedness
to the very lowliness of our humanity's clay.[4]
So that I, then,
with my littleness,   40
would be able to see your greatness,
you made yourself a little one,[5]
wrapping up the greatness of your Godhead
in the littleness of our humanity.
Thus were you revealed to us   45
in the Word,
your only-begotten Son.[6]
Thus have I come to know you,
deep well of charity,
within myself,   50
in this Word.[7]

High eternal Trinity,
boundless love,
you revealed your truth to us
in his blood.[8]   55
For then we saw your power:
that you could cleanse us of our sins
in this blood.[9]
And you revealed to us your wisdom
when you used the hook of the Godhead   60
concealed under the bait of our humanity
to catch the devil[10]
and seize from him the domination he had had over us.[11]
And this blood reveals to us your love and charity,
for it was by the fire of love alone   65
that you bought us back
even though you have no need of us.[12]
And thus your truth also is revealed to us:
that you created us
to give us eternal life.   70
This truth we have come to know
through the Word,
as I said,
whereas before we could not know it
because we had covered our mind's eye   75

with the veil of sin.
Blush,
blind creature
so honored and exalted by your God!
Blush for shame   *80*
for not recognizing
how God in his boundless charity
descended from the exaltedness of the infinite Godhead
to the lowliness of your humanity's clay
so that you might come to know him   *85*
in yourself![13]
I have sinned against the Lord.
Have mercy on me!

Oh, what a marvel it is
that, although you knew your creature   *90*
before she came into being,
and saw that she would act sinfully
and would not follow your truth,
still you created her!
O boundless love!   *95*
O boundless love!
—And to whom are you speaking, my soul?
I am speaking to you,
eternal Father;
I am pleading with you,   *100*
most gracious God:
give us and all your servants
communion in the fire of your charity,
and dispose all your creatures
to receive the fruit   *105*
of the prayers and teaching
we do and must pour out
in your light and charity.
Your Truth said,
"Seek and you shall find;   *110*
ask and it shall be given to you;
knock and it shall be opened to you."[14]
I am knocking at the door of your truth;
I am seeking and crying out
in the presence of your majesty;   *115*

I am pleading to the ears of your clemency[15]
for mercy for the whole world
and especially for holy Church.
For in the Word's teaching I have come to know
that you want me to feed constantly on this food.   120
And since this is what you want, my love,
do not let me die of hunger.

O my soul, what are you doing?
Don't you know
you are constantly seen by God?   125
Realize that you can never hide from his sight,
for nothing is hid from him.
You may well be able to hide sometimes
from creatures' eyes,
but from the Creator's,   130
never.[16]
Put a stop and an end, then,
to your evil ways,
and wake up.

I have sinned against the Lord.   135
Have mercy on me!
It is time to rise from sleep.[17]
You, eternal Trinity,
want us to wake up.
If we do not get up in time of prosperity   140
you send us adversity.
And, like a perfect doctor,
you cauterize the wound with the fire of affliction
when the ointment of comfort and prosperity
does not help.[18]   145

O eternal Father,
O uncreated charity,
I am filled with wonder
because in your light I have come to know
that you saw and knew me and all persons,   150
individually and all together,

before you ever gave us being.
You saw Adam, the first man,
and you knew the sin of disobedience
that would follow   *155*
both in him as an individual
and in the others who would come after him.
You knew that sin would be an obstacle
to your truth;
it was also an obstacle to your creatures,   *160*
since your truth was not fulfilled in them;
I mean they could not reach the goal
for which you had created them.
And you saw, eternal Father,
the suffering that would follow   *165*
for your Son
to bring humankind back to grace
and fulfill your truth in us.
In your light I have come to know
that you foresaw all these things.[19]   *170*

Why then,
eternal Father,
did you create this creature of yours?
I am truly amazed at this,
and indeed I see,   *175*
as you show me,
that you made us for one reason only:
in your light
you saw yourself compelled
by the fire of your charity   *180*
to give us being,
in spite of the evil we would commit against you,
eternal Father.
It was fire, then,
that compelled you.   *185*
O unutterable love,
even though you saw all the evils
that all your creatures would commit
against your infinite goodness,
you acted as if you did not see   *190*
and set your eye

only on the beauty of your creature,
with whom you had fallen in love
like one drunk and crazy with love.
And in love   *195*
you drew us out of yourself,
giving us being
in your own image and likeness.
You, eternal Truth,
have told me the truth: *200*
that love compelled you to create us.
Even though you saw that we would offend you,
your charity would not let you
set your eyes on that sight.
No,   *205*
you took your eyes off the sin that was to be
and fixed your gaze
only on your creature's beauty.
For if you had concentrated on the sin,
you would have forgotten the love you had   *210*
for creating humankind.
Not that the sin was hid from you,
but you concentrated on the love
because you are nothing but a fire of love,[20]
crazy over what you have made.   *215*
And I in my sinfulness
have never known you!
But give me the grace, dearest love,
that my body may give up its blood
for the honor and glory of your name.   *220*
Let me no longer be clothed in myself.

Father,
receive also the one who has given me communion
in the precious body and blood of your Son.
Strip him of himself   *225*
and free him from himself;
clothe him in your eternal will
and bind him to yourself
with a knot that can never be undone,[21]
so that he may be a fragrant plant   *230*
in the garden of holy Church.[22]

Grant, most gracious Father,
your sweet eternal benediction,
and in the blood of your Son
wash the face of our souls.   235

Love!
Love!
I beg you for death!
Amen.

NOTES

1. Most commentators have held that by "mystic body" Catherine means the clergy and hierarchy, and by "universal body," the laity. There is evidence, however (which I shall eventually publish in detail), for another interpretation. The exact basis of the distinction is not entirely apparent, but it is clear that for Catherine "mystic body" refers to the Church as a specifically sacramental reality, a reality whose whole meaning rests in the mystery of Jesus as the Sacrament of God's redeeming love, and all Christians are included in that reality by baptism.

2. Cf. Ps. 139, 1. 5: "O Lord, you have probed me and you know me. . . . Behind me and before me, you hem me in and rest your hand upon me."

3. Cf. Let. 108 (XXXXVIIII): "So strong was God's love for his creature that it moved him to draw us out of himself and give us his very own image and likeness, simply so we might taste and enjoy him and share in his eternal beauty." Also Let. 308: "When God looked within himself he fell in love with the beauty of his creature and, like one drunk with love, he created us in his own image and likeness."

4. Cf. P. 19.

5. Cf. *Dial.* 134, p. 273: "O good, O eternal greatness, you made yourself lowly and small to make us great!"

6. Cf. 1 Jn. 1, 1: "This is what we proclaim to you: what was from the beginning, what we have heard, what we have seen with our eyes, what we have looked upon and our hands have touched—we speak of the word of life."

7. Cf. Jn. 17, 26: "To them I have revealed your name, and I will continue to reveal it so that your love for me may live in them, and I may live in them."

8. The blood shed on the cross is for Catherine the clearest revelation of the mystery of God, hidden during the life of the incarnate Word like fire under ashes, and bursting into flame in his passion. This also finds an echo in P. 19. (Cavallini)

9. Cf. Eph. 1, 7: "It is in Christ and through his blood that we have been redeemed and our sins forgiven."

10. Cf. *Dial.* 135, p. 278: "So, to take away this death, dearest daughter, I gave humankind the Word, my only-begotten Son, thus providing for your need with great prudence and providence.

"I say 'with prudence' because with the bait of your humanity and the hook of my divinity I caught the devil, who could not recognize my Truth. The Truth, the incarnate Word, came to destroy and put an end to his lie, which he had used to deceive humankind."

11. Cf. Col. 2, 15: "Thus did God disarm the principalitites and powers. He made a public show of them and, leading them off captive, triumphed in the person of Christ."

12. Cf. 1 Jn. 4, 10: "Love, then, consists in this: not that we have loved God but that he has loved us and has sent his Son as an offering for our sins." Also *Dial.* 153, p. 325: "O mad lover! And you have need of your creature? It seems so to me, for you act as if you could not live without her, in spite of the fact that you are Life itself. . . ."

13. Cf. *Dial.* 12, p. 46: "Think of it! I gifted you with my image and likeness. And when you lost the life of grace through sin, to restore it to you I united my nature with you, hiding it in your humanity. I had made you in my image; now I took your image by assuming a human form."

14. Mt. 7, 7: Lk. 11, 9.

15. Truth, majesty, clemency—clearly a Trinitarian reference for Catherine, even though the usual order of Persons is inverted. (Cavallini)

16. Cf. Jer. 16, 17: "For my eyes are upon all their ways; they are not hidden from me, nor does their guilt escape my view."

17. Rom. 13, 11.

18. The contrasting images of ointment and cauterization were familiar to Catherine, in all probability from her experience as a nurse in the hospitals and homes of Siena. They recur repeatedly in both the *Dialogue* and in her *Letters.* (Cavallini)

19. Cf. 1 Pt. 1, 18–20: "Realize that you were delivered . . . not by any diminishable sum of silver or gold, but by Christ's blood beyond all price: the blood of a spotless, unblemished lamb chosen before the world's foundation and revealed for your sake in these last days."

20. Cf. Dt. 4, 24: "For the Lord, your God, is a consuming fire, a jealous God."

21. Cf. Let. 95: "I am writing to you . . . longing to see you so bound with the gentle chain of charity that neither demon nor human will be able to break it. This is the gentle chain that bound God with humanity and humanity with God . . . and this was the unutterable love that gave humanity being. . . . And because the soul was made for love alone, love gives our soul its powers. . . . Thus is it clothed in his gentle eternal will. . . . And this is the gentle chain that binds the soul to her Creator."

22. Cf. Is. 61, 10–11: "I rejoice heartily in the Lord, in my God is the joy of my soul; for he has clothed me with a robe of salvation, and wrapped me in a mantle of justice. . . . As the earth brings forth its plants, and a garden makes its

growth spring up, so will the Lord God make justice and praise spring up before all the nations." We do not know who had given Catherine communion that morning, but it must have been someone for whom she had a particular concern at the time. It is interesting to note that she had used many of the same images— fire, eating souls, undoing the knot—in a letter (329) to her disciple Stefano Maconi, then still a layman, in late January or early February.

PRAYER 14

Quinquagesima Sunday, February 20, 1379.
At Rome.

It is the Sunday before Lent (R furnishes the date), and there is a hint in Catherine's tone very early in this prayer, and again near its conclusion, that she is not entirely pleased with Pope Urban. ". . . I see that you see . . . your vicar's good will. But who is keeping him from making it effective by doing something?" There is no certain data to indicate what precise turn of events prompted the remark, yet Catherine is far more immediately preoccupied with the effects of her own sinfulness on the Church and on those for whom she is most directly responsible.

PRAYER 14

I acknowledge, eternal God;
I acknowledge, eternal God, high eternal Trinity,
that you see me and know me.
I have seen this in your light.
I acknowledge, eternal God,   5
and I see
that you see your bride's need
and your vicar's good will.
But who is keeping him
from making it effective by doing something?   10
In your light I have seen
that you know these things,
for nothing is hid from your eyes.[1]

In this light I see
that you foresaw within yourself   15
the help you eventually gave
to this dead child of yours, humankind—
and that help was the Word,
your only-begotten Son.
And you foresaw as well   20
something else that would help this dead child:
preserving the scars in the Word's body
so that these might continually cry out
in your presence
for mercy for us.[2]   25
In your light I have seen
that it was the fire of love
that made you preserve these wounds,
and his glorified body no more interferes
with his wounds   30
or the color of his blood
than these impede
the glorification of his body.

You saw too within yourself
that, even after you had freed us from our sickness,   35
we would still fall into sin every day
because of our weakness.
So you gave us help for this
in the sacrament of holy penance,
where the minister pours over the soul's face   40
the blood of the humble Lamb.[3]
Just as you saw that our chief help
lay in reconciling us to yourself
through the Word,
so also you saw all these other helps   45
we would need for our salvation.
In your light I know
that you saw all these things in advance.
For it is in this light that I see,
and without this light   50
I would be walking in darkness.[4]

O most tender love,
you saw within yourself
your holy Church's need
and the help she has to have,   55
and you have given it to her
in the form of your servants' prayers,
of which you choose to make a buttress
to support the wall of holy Church.[5]
And your mercy,   60
the Holy Spirit,
serves these servants of yours
with blazing desires for this Church's reform.

I see too
that you saw that perverse law in us   65
that is always ready to rebel against your will,
and you saw
that we would often follow that law.[6]
Truly I see
that you saw the weakness of this human nature of ours,   70

how weak and frail and poor it is.
This is why,
supreme provider
who have provided for your creature in everything,
and best of helpers   75
who have given us help for every need—
this is why you gave us
the strong citadel of our will[7]
as a partner for this weakness of our flesh.
For our will is so strong   80
that neither the devil nor any other creature
can conquer it
unless we so choose—
unless free choice,
in whose hand this strength has been put,   85
consents to it.[8]

O infinite goodness!
Where is the source of such strength
in your creature's will?
In you,   90
supreme and eternal strength!
So I see
that our will shares in the strength of yours,
for out of your will
you gave us ours.   95
So we see that our will is strong
to the extent that it follows yours,
and it is weak
to the extent that it departs from yours.
For, as I have said,   100
out of your own will you created ours,
and therefore ours is strong
when it dwells in yours.
All these things I have seen
in your light.   105
In our will,
eternal Father,
you reveal the strength of your will.
For if you have given such strength
to a tiny member,   110

how great should we reckon your own to be—
you who are creator and ruler of all things!

One thing I see in your light:
this will, which you have given us as free,
seems to receive its strength   *115*
from the light of faith,
for by this light
we come in your light to know your eternal will,
and we see that your will wants nothing else
but that we be made holy.[9]   *120*
So the light strengthens the will
and makes it grow,
and the will,
nourished by the light of holy faith,
gives life to our human actions.   *125*
So there can be neither a true will
nor a living faith
without action.[10]
This light of faith
nourishes the fire within the soul   *130*
and makes it grow,
for we cannot feel the fire of your charity
unless the light shows us
your love and affection for us.
You, light,   *135*
are also the fuel for the fire,
since it is you
that make the fire grow in the soul.
Just as wood makes a material fire grow
and become more intense,   *140*
you, light, are the fuel
that makes charity grow in the soul,
for you show the soul the divine goodness.
And charity in turn nourishes you,
for charity desires to know its God   *145*
and you want to satisfy it.[11]

O best of providers,
you did not want humankind to walk in darkness

or to live in war,
so you furnished us with the light of faith   *150*
to show us the way
and give us peace and tranquility.
This light does not allow the soul
to die of hunger
or go about naked or poor,   *155*
for it feeds her with the food of grace,
letting her enjoy the food of souls,[12]
clothing her in the wedding garment
of perfect charity and of your eternal will,
opening up before her   *160*
eternal wealth.[13]

I have sinned against the Lord.
Have mercy on me,
for the darkness of the perverse law
that I have always followed   *165*
has clouded my mind's eye
and so I have not known you, true light.
Yet it has pleased your charity,
true light,
to enlighten me with yourself.   *170*

O God eternal,
O boundless love!
Your creatures have been wholly kneaded into you
and you into us—[14]
through creation,   *175*
through the will's strength,
through the fire with which you created us,
and through the natural light you gave us,
the light by which we see you, true light,
if we put it to use   *180*
in hunger for true solid virtue
for the glory and praise of your name.
O light above every light!
O goodness above every goodness!
O wisdom above every wisdom!   *185*
O fire transcending every fire!

For you alone are the one who is;
none other is anything at all
except in so far as that other has being from you.

O my wretched blind soul,   *190*
unworthy to be taken with God's other servants
to be made into a wall to support holy Church!
You are worthy rather
to be planted in some beast's belly,
for you have always acted like a beast.[15]   *195*
Thanks,
thanks to you, eternal God,
that you have seen fit to choose me for this work
in spite of my sins.

I beg you, then: *200*
Since you breathe into the spirits of your servants
eager and blazing desires
for the reform of your bride
and make them cry out with continual prayer,[16]
listen to their cry.   *205*
Preserve and intensify your vicar's good will,
and let the true perfection you require of him
be realized in him.
I ask the same for all people,
and most especially   *210*
for those you have put on my shoulders.
I give them back to you,
since I am weak and inadequate.[17]
I do not want my sins
to be an obstacle for them,   *215*
since I have always followed that perverse law.
Rather I desire and I pray
that they may follow you perfectly,
so that the prayers they offer
and must offer to you   *220*
for all the world
and for holy Church
may deserve to be heard.

I have sinned against the Lord,
Have mercy on me! 225
forgive me, Father;
forgive me,
wretched and ungrateful as I have been
for the countless graces I have received from you.
I acknowledge that your goodness 230
has preserved me as your bride,
even though I by my sins
have been constantly unfaithful to you.
I have sinned against the Lord.
Have mercy on me! 235
Amen.

NOTES

1. Cf. Sir. 39, 19: "The works of all humankind are present to him; not a thing escapes his eye."

2. Cf. Rom. 8, 34: "Who shall condemn them? Christ Jesus, who died or rather was raised up, who is at the right hand of God and who intercedes for us?" Heb. 7, 25: ". . . he forever lives to make intercession for them." Cf. also S. *Th.* III, q. 54, a. 4.

3. Cf. *Dial.* 75, p. 138: "There is a second way the soul receives this baptism of blood, figuratively speaking. This my divine charity provided because I know how people sin because of their weakness. . . . So my divine charity had to leave them an ongoing baptism of blood accessible by heartfelt contrition and a holy confession as soon as they can confess to my ministers who hold the key to the blood. This blood the priest pours over the soul in absolution."

4. Cf. Ps. 36, 10: ". . . in your light we see light." Jn. 12, 35: "The light is among you only a little longer. Walk while you still have it or darkness will come over you."

5. Cf. 1 Pt. 2, 5: "You too are living stones, built as an edifice of spirit. . . ." The image could well have been inspired by the buttresses of Gothic architecture familiar to Catherine, or possibly by the legend of Pope Innocent III's dream of St. Dominic holding up the tottering walls of the Lateran Basilica.

6. Cf. Rom. 7, 22–23: "My inner self agrees with the law of God, but I see in my body's members another law at war with the law of the mind; this makes me the prisoner of the law of sin in my members."

7. Cf. Let. 335: "God's servants . . . are not bothered by toil, but are concerned only to hold the strong citadel of their will. . . ."

8. The soul is a city with three main gates: memory, understanding, and will. Of these three, "only the gate of the will is within our freedom, and it has

for its guard free choice. This gate is so strong that neither the devil nor any other creature can open it unless the guard consents. And so long as this gate is not opened by consenting to what memory and understanding and the other gates feel, our city is forever free." (Let 319).

9. Cf. *Dial.* 167, p. 365: "In the light of faith I gain wisdom in the wisdom of the Word your Son; in the light of faith I am strong, constant, persevering; in the light of faith I have hope. . . ." 1 Thes. 4, 3: "It is God's will that you grow in holiness."

10. Cf. Jas. 2, 17, 26: "So it is with the faith that does nothing in practice. It is thoroughly lifeless. . . . Be assured, then, that faith without works is dead as a body without breath."

11. Cf. *Dial.* 85, p. 157: "In that charity they receive supernatural light, and in that light they love me. For love follows upon understanding. The more they know, the more they love, and the more they love, the more they know. Thus each nourishes the other."

12. The Italian text has *food of the soul,* while the Latin has *food of souls,* meaning "the food which is souls." For Catherine the two are equivalent, since for her, apostolic zeal is "feeding on souls at the table of the cross."

13. Cf. *Dial.* 135–136, p. 277ff.

14. Cf. P. 18, where, in reference to the incarnation of the Word, Catherine prays, "Today the Godhead is joined and kneaded into one dough with our humanity. . . ." The image, often repeated in Catherine's writings, is one of total interpenetration, such as that of the yeast in the dough. It also plays into her total sacramental and eucharistic symbolism.

15. A severe self-condemnation, not unlike those leveled against the evil clergy in *Dial.* 123–126, p. 235ff. It is a reflection of Catherine's profound sense of her own sinfulness and of her responsibility, at least indirectly, for all sin. It reflects also, in its drastic contrast, her intense desire for identification with the redemptive mission of Christ. Cf. Let. 295, written to Raymond of Capua after her narrow escape from martyrdom (or rather, its escape from her) in Florence the previous summer: "So I must weep, for so great is the multitude of my sins that I have not deserved to have my blood be life-giving . . . nor to lay a stone with my blood into the wall of the mystic body of holy Church."

16. Cf. *Dial.* 66, p. 126: ". . . holy desire, that is, having a good and holy will, is continual prayer."

17. The reference is to Catherine's disciples. Cf. also one of her last prayers, recorded by Barduccio Canigiani (in Gigli, *Opere di S. Caterina da Siena,* 1707, vol. 1, p. 486): "O unhappy me! You appointed me as a guide of souls, entrusting to me so many dear children for me to love with a special love, and to guide to you along the path of life. But I have been nothing to them but a mirror of human weakness. Nor have I had a conscientious concern for them, or supported them with continual humble prayer in your presence. Nor have I given them adequate example of a good life, or the counsels of sound teaching."

PRAYER 15

Shrove Tuesday, February 22, 1379.
At Rome.

The themes of Lent are clearly on Catherine's mind as she prays on this last day of the typically licentious revelry of Carnival (the date is provided by R).

PRAYER 15

O God eternal!
O God eternal!
Have compassion on us!
You, high eternal Trinity, say
that compassion blossoming in mercy   5
is your hallmark
(for mercy is proper to you,
and mercy never lacks compassion,
so it is through compassion
that you have mercy on us).   10
I agree.
For through compassion alone
you gave up the Word your Son to death
for our redemption.
And that compassion sprang,   15
as from a fountain,
from the love with which you had created
your creature.¹
This creature was so pleasing to you
that when she lost the garment of innocence   20
you were moved to clothe her once more in your grace
by leading her back
to where she had been before.
You did not make her incapable of sin,
but left her with her free choice   25
and the perverse law
that constantly fights against the spirit,
the law that sets her up
to fall into sin's guilt
if she follows it.²   30

Since you, God eternal,
are so compassionate,³
why is it that human beings
are so cruel to themselves?
For there is no greater cruelty   35

they can do themselves
than to kill themselves
with the guilt of deadly sin.
On their sensuality they have compassion—
a compassion that inflicts great cruelty   40
on both body and soul,
since the bodies of the damned
will be punished along with their souls.[4]
I see that this has no other source
but their unenlightened being,   45
for they have not known your compassion for us.
This is why you show us
that your compassion will avail us not at all
unless we ourselves are compassionate.
And from this it is clear   50
that, though you created us without our help,
you do not want to save us without our help.[5]
You want us,
merciful and compassionate Father,
to look at your boundless compassion for us,   55
so that we may learn to be compassionate,
first of all to ourselves
and then to our neighbors—
just as the glorious Paul said,
"All charity begins with oneself."[6]   60
So you want the soul to look at your compassion
so that she may rise above her own cruelty
and accept the food your compassion offers
to nourish her and give her life.[7]

O God eternal!   65
O fire and deep well of charity!
Your eyes are upon us.
And you have given us the eye of understanding
so that your creature might see that this is so:
that you have either   70
the eyes of your mercy and compassion
or the eyes of your justice
set upon us,
according to our actions.[8]
So it is perfectly clear   75

that every evil comes of our being unenlightened,
and every good comes to us from the light.[9]
For we cannot love
what we do not know,
and we can know nothing   80
without the light.[10]
O eternal God!
O compassionate, O merciful Father!
Have compassion and mercy on us,
for we are blind   85
and have no light at all—
and I, poor wretch that I am,
am blindest of all,
and so I have been constantly cruel to myself.
With that eye of compassion   90
with which you created us and everything,[11]
look at the world's need
and provide for it.
You gave us being out of nothingness;
enlighten, then,   95
this being which is your own.
You gave us the light of the apostles
when we needed it;
now, when we have even greater need of light,
raise up another Paul   100
to enlighten the whole world.
Cover and blind the eye of your justice
with mercy's veil
and open the eye of your compassion.
With charity's chain   105
bind yourself[12]
and calm your anger.

O sweet gentle light!
O principle and foundation of our salvation!
Because in the light you saw our need,   110
in this same light we see your eternal goodness,
and knowing it
we love it.
O union and bond
of you our Creator   115

with your creature,
and of your creature
with you our Creator![13]
With the cord of your charity
you have bound us,   120
and in your light
you have given us light.[14]
So if we open the eye of our understanding
with a will to know you,
we know you,   125
for your light enters into every soul
who opens the gate of her will.
For the light stands at the soul's gate,
and as soon as the gate is opened to it,
the light enters,[15]   130
just like the sun
that knocks at the shuttered window
and, as soon as it is opened,
comes into the house.
So the soul has to have a will to know,   135
and with that will
she has to open her understanding's eye,[16]
and then you, true Sun, enter the soul
and flood her with the light that is yourself.
And once you have entered,   140
what do you do,
light of compassion,
within the soul?
You dispel the darkness
and give her light.[17]   145
You draw out of her the dampness of selfish love
and leave her the fire of your charity.
You make her heart free,
for in your light she has come to know
what great liberty you have given us   150
by snatching us
from the slavery to the devil
into which we humans had come
because of our own cruelty,[18]
and so she hates the cause of the cruelty,   155
that is, compassion for selfish sensuality,
and therefore she becomes compassionate toward reason

and cruel against sensuality
by closing her powers to it.
She closes her memory   160
to the mean things of the world
and to empty pleasures,
willingly taking away from it
the remembrance of these things,
and opens it to your blessings,   165
pondering these with good care.
She closes her will
so that it loves nothing outside of you,
but loves you above all things
and everything in you   170
according to your will,
and wants only to follow you.[19]
Then she is truly compassionate to herself,
and just as she is compassionate to herself,
so is she to her neighbors,   175
ready to give up her bodily life
for the salvation of souls.
In all things she exercises compassion
with prudence
because she has seen with what great prudence   180
you have worked all your mysteries in us.[20]

You, light, make the heart simple,
not two-faced.
You make it big,
not stingy—   185
so big that it has room in its loving charity
for everyone:
with well-ordered charity
it seeks everyone's salvation,
and because light is never without prudence   190
and wisdom,
it is ready to give its body up to death
for the salvation of a neighbor's soul,
but will not give its soul up to sin—
for we are not allowed to commit the least sin   195
even to save the whole world
(if that were possible),

since it is not right to offend the Creator,
who is all good,
for the benefit of creatures,   200
who are nothing by themselves.
But for a neighbor's physical good,
such a heart will give up its material possessions.[21]
Such a heart is so open
that it is false to no one;   205
everyone can understand it
because it never says something different
with its face or tongue
from what it has within.
It shows that is has truly been stripped   210
of its old garment
and is clothed in the new garment
of your will.[22]
So our cruelty, eternal Father,
springs from our failure to see   215
the compassion you have shown our souls
by buying them back
with your only-begotten Son's precious blood.

Turn, merciful Father,
turn the eye of your compassion   220
on your bride
and on your vicar.
Hide him under the wings of your mercy[23]
so that the wicked and the proud
may not harm him.   225
And grant me the grace to pour out my blood
and scatter the marrow of my bones
in this garden, holy Church.
If I look into you   230
I see that nothing is hid from your eyes.
Worldly people
whose eyes are blinded by the cloud of selfish love
do not see this,
for if they saw it   235
they would not be so cruel
to their own souls.
No,

in your compassion
they would become compassionate.   240
This is why we need the light—
and with all the feeling that is in me
I beg you to give this light
to all people.
In the Word   245
you exercised compassion and justice:
justice on his body
and compassion on your creatures![24]
O infinite goodness!
Why doesn't the human heart melt?   250
Why doesn't my heart spill out in my voice?
Because the cloud has darkened my spirit's vision
and keeps you, my soul,
from seeing this unutterable compassion.[25]
What father ever give up his own son to death   255
for his slave?[26]
Only you, eternal Father.
Our flesh,
in which you clothed the Word,
suffered   260
and we receive the fruit of it
if we but choose to.
In the same way
you want our sensuality to suffer
so that the soul may receive the fruit of life.   265
O teaching rooted in truth!
This is why your Truth said,
"I am Way,
Truth,
and Life."[27]   270
If we want to follow your compassion
we have no choice
but to walk the way
that you walked freely.
I am indicting myself, eternal Truth,   275
so that you may pass sentence on me,
for I am cruel to my soul
and compassionate to my selfish sensuality![28]
I have sinned against the Lord.
Have mercy on me!   280

O compassionate cruelty!
You trample sensuality to the ground
in this finite time
so that you may raise the soul up
for ever!   285
What is the source of patience?
What the source of faith,
of hope,
of charity?
The same compassion   290
that gives birth to mercy.
What frees the soul from herself
and binds her to you?
This compassion
achieved in the light.   295
O lovely compassion!
O compassion,
you are a balm
that snuffs out rage and cruelty in the soul.
This compassion,   300
compassionate Father,
I beg you to give to all your creatures,
especially to those you have given me
to love with a special love.
Make them compassionate,   305
that they may exercise perfect compassion
as well as perfect cruelty
to kill their evil will.
This is the compassionate cruelty
that you, Truth, seemed to be teaching us when you said,   310
"If you come to me
without hating father and mother,
spouse and children,
brothers and sisters,
and even your own soul,   315
you cannot be my disciple."[29]
The first of these
the world's servants often hate,
though not for love of virtue.
The last, however, seems difficult.   320
But it is not really difficult:
it is more difficult

to go contrary to one's own nature
than to follow it,
and our nature is reasonable,   325
so we ought to follow reason.

O eternal Truth!
Fragrance above every fragrance!
Generosity beyond all generosity!
Compassion beyond all compassion!   330
Justice beyond all justice!
Even more:
you are the very fountain of justice
rewarding each of us
according to our deeds.[30]   335
So you let the wicked
become insupportable to themselves
because they set their hearts
on what is less than themselves,
hankering after worldly pleasures and wealth.   340
For all created things
are less than the human person;
they were made to serve us,
not for us to make ourselves their slaves.[31]
Only you   345
are greater than we;
therefore it is you we should desire,
seek,
and serve.
Justly   350
you let the just have in this life
a foretaste of eternal life
in spiritual peace and calm,
since they have set their hearts on you
who are true and supreme calm.   355
And to those
who have run the course of this mortal life
with courage
you give eternal life
with justice and mercy.   360
You are eternal infinite goodness.
No one can fully know or understand you

except as you grant that knowledge,[32]
and you grant us
as much as we open the vessel of our soul   365
to receive.
O most tender love!
In the whole of my life's time
I have never known you,
and so I have never loved you.   370

I commend to you my children
whom you have put on my shoulders.
You commissioned me to keep them awake—
me, who am always sleeping!
Wake them up yourself,   375
kind and compassionate Father,
so that the eyes of their understanding
may always be wide awake
in you.

I have sinned against the Lord.   380
Have mercy on me!
God, come to our assistance;
Lord, make haste to help us!
Amen.

NOTES

1. Cf. Jer. 31, 3: "With age-old love I have loved you; so I have kept my mercy toward you."

2. Cf. Rom. 7, 21–23; Gal. 5, 17: "The flesh lusts against the spirit and the spirit against the flesh; the two are directly opposed."

3. Cf. 2 Chr. 30, 9: ". . . merciful and compassionate is the Lord, your God." Sir. 2, 11: "Compassionate and merciful is the Lord."

4. Cf. Mt. 10, 28: "Do not fear those who deprive the body of life but cannot destroy the soul. Rather, fear him who can destroy both body and soul in Gehenna."

5. St. Augustine, Sermon 169, 11, 13. (Cavallini)

6. The reference is not directly Pauline; I have not been able to trace its source, but the literature seems to indicate that sayings similar to "Charity be-

gins at home" and "You are your own nearest neighbor" are quoted as proverbial already centuries ago. Cf. *Dial.* 11, p. 44: "I am supreme eternal Truth. So discernment sets neither law nor limit nor condition to the love it gives me. But it rightly sets conditions and priorities of love where other people are concerned. . . . So you see, every soul desirous of grace loves me—as she ought—without limit or condition. And with my own infinite love she loves her neighbors with the measured and ordered charity I have described, never bringing on herself the evil of sin in doing good for others. Saint Paul taught you this when he said that charity cannot fully profit others unless it begins with oneself. For when perfection is not in the soul, whatever she does, whether for herself or for others, is imperfect." (Cf. 1 Cor. 13, 1–3.)

7. Cf. Let. 265: "Learn from this spent and slain Lamb how . . . he set himself to eating with pleasure the food of his Father's honor and our salvation at the table of the shameful cross, ignoring his own exhaustion and anguish. . . . Who is there with a heart so mean that it could look at this knight and captain who was victorious even when dead, and not rise above his or her own weakness and become courageous in the face of any adversary? No one! This is why I told you to set Christ crucified before you as the object of your contemplation." Cf. also *Dial.* 51, p. 103f.

8. Cf. Ps. 34, 16–17: "The Lord has eyes for the just, and ears for their cry. The Lord confronts the evildoers, to destroy remembrance of them from the earth."

9. St. Thomas Aquinas, *Super Ev. S. Ioannis Lect.*, 122: "Our salvation consists in this, that we have a share in the light itself."

10. Cf. Let. 113: "Since we needed light, God provides for our need by giving us the light of understanding, the most noble part of the soul, with most holy faith at its center as its pupil. . . . The soul, made of love and created for love in God's image and likeness, cannot live without love, nor love without light. If she wants to love, then, she must see. . . . Without loving and without seeing it is impossible to live."

11. *S. Th.* I, q. 21, a. 4.

12. Cf. *Dial.* 143, p. 297: "It is love that constrains me, because I loved you before you came to be. . . . This is what constrains me to do it, along with the prayers of my servants. . . . They spare no effort to placate my wrath and tie the hands of my divine justice, which the wicked deserve to have me employ against them."

13. Cf. Let. 7: "Charity is the gentle holy chain that binds the soul with her Creator. It binds God with humankind, and humankind with God. This boundless charity held the God-man fixed and nailed to the wood of the most holy cross."

14. Cf. Ps. 36, 10: ". . . in your light we see light."

15. Cf. Rv. 3, 20: "Here I stand, knocking at the door. If you hear me calling and open the door I will enter your house. . . ." Here, as in P. 18, Catherine emphasizes the delicacy of God's action. He will never force our will, but stands waiting like a beggar at the door, until we freely open ourselves to his light. (Cavallini)

16. Cf. St. Thomas Aquinas, *De Malo,* q. 6, r.

17. Cf. Jb. 12, 22: "The recesses of the darkness he discloses, and brings the gloom forth to the light." 2 Cor. 4, 6: "For God, who said, 'Let light shine out of darkness,' has shone in our hearts, that we in turn might make known the glory of God shining on the face of Christ."

18. Cf. Jn. 8, 31–36: "If you live according to my teaching . . . you will know the truth, and the truth will set you free. . . . I give you my assurance, everyone who lives in sin is the slave of sin." 2 Cor. 3, 17: ". . . where the Spirit of the Lord is, there is freedom."

19. This passage is a sort of amplification, from a positive point of view, of the description of the soul as a city with three main gates (memory, understanding, and will). Where this image is treated in the *Dialogue* (144, p. 299ff.) the will opens to sin, with evil consequences for the soul's other powers. Here the will opens to light, with consequential good effects in the other powers. In this passage, moreover, the enlightened understanding is given a special prominence that the negative scenario of the *Dialogue* passage did not allow for. (Cavallini)

20. Cf. *Dial.* 135, p. 278: "So, to take away this death . . . I gave humankind the Word, my only-begotten Son, thus providing for your need with great prudence and providence."

21. Cf. Let. 254: "Love would be disordered that would commit sin to save oneself or to please one's neighbor. . . . Well-ordered love in God would not choose to give up one's soul to save even the whole world. . . . But one certainly ought to give up one's bodily life for the soul of one's neighbor, and one's material possessions to save one's neighbor's body." *Dial.* 11, p. 44: "The light of discernment, which is born of charity, gives order to your love for your neighbors. It would not permit you to bring the guilt of sin on yourself to benefit your neighbor. For that love would indeed be disordered and lacking in discernment which would commit even a single sin to redeem the whole world from hell or to achieve one great virtue. No, neither the greatest of virtues nor any service to your neighbor may be bought at the price of sin. The priorities set by holy discernment direct all the soul's powers to serving me courageously and conscientiously. Then she must love her neighbors with such affection that she would bear any pain or torment to win them the life of grace, ready to die a thousand deaths, if that were possible, for their salvation. And all her material possessions are at the service of her neighbors' physical needs. Such is the work of the light of discernment born of charity." Cf. also St. Thomas Aquinas, *De Caritate,* a. 11.

22. Cf. Col. 3, 9–10: "Stop lying to one another. What you have done is put aside your old self with its past deeds and put on a new self, one that grows in knowledge as it is formed anew in the image of its Creator."

23. Cf. Ps. 17, 8: "Hide me in the shadow of your wings." (This verse was surely very familiar to Catherine from Compline.) Ps. 61, 5: "Oh, that I might lodge in your tent forever, take refuge in the shelter of your wings!" (Cavallini)

24. Cf. *Dial.* 14, p. 52: ". . . I really wanted to restore you, incapable as you were of making atonement for yourself. And because you were so utterly handicapped, I sent the Word, my Son; I clothed him with the same nature as yours—the spoiled clay of Adam—so that he could suffer in that same nature

which had sinned, and by suffering in his body even to the extent of the shameful death on the cross he would placate my anger. And so I satisfied both my justice and my divine mercy."

25. Cf. Let. 350: "What deprives us of this true and gentle light? Our selfish love for ourselves, which is a cloud that darkens the eye of our understanding and covers over its pupil, most holy faith."

26. Cf. Rom. 8, 32: ". . . he who did not spare his own Son but handed him over for the sake of us all. . . ." Also the *Exultet* for the Easter Vigil: "To redeem a slave you gave up your only Son."

27. Jn. 14, 6.

28. Cf. Eph. 2, 3: ". . . we lived at the level of the flesh, following every whim and fancy, and so by nature deserved God's wrath like the rest."

29. Lk. 14, 26.

30. Cf. Ps. 62, 13: ". . . yours, O Lord, is kindness; and you render to all according to their deeds."

31. Cf. *Dial.* 48, p. 98ff. for a development of this.

32. Cf. Mt. 11, 27: "No one knows the Son but the Father, and no one knows the Father but the Son—and anyone to whom the Son wishes to reveal him."

PRAYER 16

Tuesday, March 1, 1379.[1]
At Rome.

This prayer was recorded just a week after the previous one, on the Tuesday after the First Sunday of Lent, and its theme is again characteristic of the season.

A postscript to the text indicates that the conclusion—the more personal part—has been left out.

PRAYER 16

Eternal Trinity!
O high eternal Trinity!
You, eternal Trinity,
gave us the gentle loving Word.
O gentle loving word,   5
God's Son,
your nature is as strong
and ready for every good
as ours is weak
and ready for every evil.   10
We are weak
because we have received our parents' weak nature.
Now parents cannot give their children
a nature other than their own,
and that nature is inclined to evil   15
because of the rebelliousness of their weak flesh,
which they in turn
have received from their parents.
So our nature is weak
and ready for every evil   20
because we are all descendants and offspring
of our first father, Adam,
and we have all come
from the same clay.[2]
Because Adam broke away from you,   25
eternal Father,
supreme strength,
he became weak.
Because he rebelled against you,
he found rebellion within himself.[3]   30
So, once he had broken away
from your supreme goodness and strength,
he discovered that he was weak
and ready for every evil.

O Word,   35
God's eternal Son,

your nature is strong
and ready for every good
because you received it
from your eternal all-powerful Father.   40
He gave you his nature,
divinity.
No evil was or could be in you
because the nature you received from the Godhead
could suffer no defect.   45
You, therefore, gentle Word,
have strengthened our weak nature
by your becoming one with us.
Our nature has been strengthened by this union
because by the power of your blood   50
its weakness is canceled out
in holy baptism.
And when we have reached the age of discernment
we are further strengthened
by your teaching   55
Those who follow it in truth
and clothe themselves in it completely
become so strong and ready for good
that they all but lose
the rebelliousness of their flesh   60
against the spirit.
For such souls
are perfectly one with your teaching,
and their body is so one with their soul
that it wants to follow the soul's lead.   65
It even reaches a point
at which the things they used to enjoy—
the wretched pleasures of the world—
now thoroughly disgust them,
and the pursuit of virtue,   70
which before seemed to them hard and difficult,
is now sweet and delightful to them.[4]
So it is true indeed
that you, eternal Word,
canceled out our nature's weakness   75
by the strength of your nature,
which you received from the Father.
You have given us this strength

(as I have said)
through your blood
and through your teaching.   *80*

O eternal blood!
(I say eternal
because you are united with the divine nature.)
When we have come   *85*
by the light
to know your strength,
we break away from our own weakness.
But unless we hate our selfish sensuality,
not only can we never have this light,   *90*
but we lose the natural light as well.[5]

O sweet blood!
You strengthen the soul;
you enlighten her;
in you she becomes like an angel.   *95*
You so engulf her
in your charity's fire
that she completely forgets herself
and can see nothing but you.
Even her weak flesh   *100*
senses the fragrance of virtue—
so much so
that it seems that body and soul
cry out to you in unison
in whatever she does.   *105*
This is true
so long as she stands firm in holy desire
and continues to grow in it,
for if she would let her desire relax,
the rebelliousness of her flesh would reawaken   *110*
more alive than ever.[6]

O teaching of truth!
You give such strength
to the soul clothed in you

that neither difficulty nor pain　　　　　　　　　　*115*
can make her fall.
In every struggle she is victorious.
You come from strength itself,
so as long as she follows you
she is strong.　　　　　　　　　　　　　　　　*120*
But your strength would be of no use to her at all
if she did not follow you.[7]
Woe is me
that I have never followed you,
true teaching!　　　　　　　　　　　　　　　　*125*
I am therefore so weak
that I fall at every least difficulty.
I have sinned against the Lord.
Have mercy on me!

THEN SHE PRAYED FOR HOLY CHURCH,　　　*130*
FOR CHRIST'S VICAR,
FOR THE WHOLE WORLD,
AND ESPECIALLY FOR HER CHILDREN IN CHRIST,
IN HER USUAL WAY, WITH THE MOST TENDER,
LOFTY, AND BEAUTIFUL WORDS—
WHICH I PASS OVER.

NOTES

1. R gives the date as March 1 "of the same year." A and G both specify the day as Monday, which Cavallini points out must be an error, since March 1 fell on Tuesday in 1379.

2. Cf. Rom. 5, 12: ". . . through one man sin entered the world and with sin death, death thus coming to all inasmuch as all sinned. . . ."

3. Cf. *Dial.* 21, p. 58: "My creatures found rebellion within themselves, for as soon as they rebelled against me, they became rebels against themselves. Their innocence lost, the flesh rebelled against the spirit and they became filthy beasts. All created things rebelled against them, whereas they would have been submissive if all had been kept as I had established it in the beginning."

4. For a development of this, see *Dial.* 126–128, p. 244ff.

5. Cf. *Dial.* 46, pp. 94–95: "Because they know neither me nor themselves, they do not hate their selfish sensuality. No, they even love it. . . . You see, then, that they are deluded. Who has deluded them? None but themselves, for

they have thrown away the light of living faith, and they go about as if they were blind, groping and clutching at everything they touch."

6. Cf. *Dial.* 145, p. 305: "Sometimes I resort to a pleasant trick with them to keep them humble. I make their feelings fall asleep so that it seems to them they feel nothing either in their will or their emotions, as if they were asleep though not, I say, dead. For the sensual emotions slumber in the perfect soul but they do not die. This is why, if they relax their efforts or let the flame of holy desire grow dim, these emotions will awaken stronger than ever." Also 1 Cor. 10, 12: ". . . let those who think they are standing upright watch out lest they fall!"

7. Cf. Mt. 7, 21: "None of those who cry out, 'Lord, Lord,' will enter the kingdom of God but only those who do the will of my Father in heaven."

PRAYER 17

Thursday, March 3, 1379.
At Rome.

Only two days have passed since the preceding prayer (R provides the date).

Particularly noteworthy here, as in the previous prayer and elsewhere, is Catherine's interpretation of the double gift we receive in Christ: his blood and his teaching, both of which call us to an active response. This sacramentality of the Word is very central to Catherine's spirituality: we are not truly redeemed except as we enter into the redemptive way of living patterned for us by Jesus in all that he did and said.

PRAYER 17

High eternal Trinity!
O Trinity, eternal Godhead!
Love!
We are trees of death
and you are the tree of life.[1]   5
O eternal Godhead!
What a wonder,
in your light,
to see your creature as a pure tree,
a tree you drew out of yourself,   10
supreme purity,
in pure innocence!
You planted it and fused it
into the humanity you had formed
from the earth's clay.[2]   15
You made this tree free.
You gave it branches:
the soul's powers
of memory,
understanding,   20
and will.
With what fruit did you endow the memory?
With the fruit of holding.
And understanding?
With the fruit of discerning.   25
And the will?
With the fruit of loving.
O tree
set in such purity
by the one who planted you!   30

But this tree broke away from innocence:
it fell in disobedience
and from a tree of life
became a tree of death,

so that it no longer produced any fruits   35
but those of death.[3]
And you,
high eternal Trinity,
acted as if you were drunk with love,
infatuated with your creature.   40
When you saw that this tree could bear no fruit
but the fruit of death
because it was cut off from you who are life,
you came to its rescue
with the same love   45
with which you had created it:
you engrafted your divinity
into the dead tree of our humanity.
O sweet tender engrafting!
You, sweetness itself,   50
stooped to join yourself
with our bitterness.
You, splendor,
joined yourself with darkness;
you, wisdom,   55
with foolishness;
you, life,
with death;
you, the infinite,
with us who are finite.   60
What drove you to this
to give back life to this creature of yours
that had so insulted you?
Only love,
as I have said,   65
and so by this engrafting,
death is destroyed.[4]

And was it enough for your charity
to have effected such a union with your creature?
No.   70
So you, eternal Word,
watered this tree with your blood.[5]
With its warmth

this blood makes the tree bear fruit,
if only we use our free choice   75
to engraft ourselves into you,
to join and make one with you
our heart and affection,
binding and wrapping the graft
with the band of charity   80
and following your teaching.
Now we neither should nor can follow the Father,
because no suffering can befall him.[6]
We must conform ourselves to you
through suffering and anguished desires.   85
So through you who are life
we will produce the fruit of life
if we choose to engraft ourselves into you.
It is clear then
that though you created us without our help,   90
you do not want to save us without our help.

Once we have been engrafted into you,
the branches you gave our tree
begin to produce their fruit.
Our memory is filled   95
with the continual recollection of your blessings.
Our understanding gazes into you
to know perfectly your truth
and your will.
And our will chooses to love and to follow   100
what our understanding has seen and known.
So each branch offers its fruit to the others.[7]
And because of our knowledge of you
we know ourselves better
and hate ourselves—   105
I mean we hate our selfish sensuality.

O love, immeasurable love,
wonderful are the things you have wrought
in your reasoning creature!
And if, God eternal,   110

you made us into trees of life again
when we were trees of death
by engrafting yourself, life,
into us
(though many because of their sins   *115*
produce only fruits of death
because they do not engraft themselves
into you, eternal life[8]),
then you can provide now too
for the salvation of everyone   *120*
I see today
refusing to engraft themselves into you.
In fact, most of them
are persisting in their death
of selfish sensuality,   *125*
and none of them come to the fountain
where there is the blood
to water their trees.

Oh,
within us is eternal life,   *130*
and we do not know it!
O my poor blind soul,
where is your crying?
Where are the tears you ought to be shedding[9]
in the sight of your God   *135*
who is constantly inviting you?[10]
Where is your heartfelt sorrow
for the trees who remain planted in death;
where are your anguished desires
in the presence of divine compassion?[11]   *140*
These things are not in me
because I still have not lost myself.[12]
For if I had lost myself
and had sought only God
and the glory and praise of his name,   *145*
my heart would pour itself out in my voice
and my bones would weep out their marrow.
But I have never produced anything
but the fruit of death
because I have not engrafted myself into you.   *150*

What light,
what nobility
does the soul receive
who is in truth engrafted into you?
O immeasurable generosity!   *155*
Memory offers us the reminder
that we are bound and obliged to love you
and to follow the teaching and example
of the Word, your only-begotten Son.
But without the light of faith   *160*
we cannot follow Christ's teaching and example,
so understanding fixes its gaze in this light
in order to know,
and the will in its turn
loves what understanding has seen and known.   *165*
Thus does each branch
offer its fruit of life to the others.

And from what source,
O tree—
since of yourself you are dead and barren—   *170*
do you get these fruits of life?
From the tree of life—13
for unless you were engrafted into him
you would have no power
to produce any fruit at all,   *175*
because you are nothing.

O eternal Truth!
Boundless love!
You brought forth fruits for us:
the fire of love,   *180*
light,
and ready obedience.
In that obedience
you ran as one in love
to the shameful death of the cross,   *185*
and you gave us these fruits
through the engrafting of your divinity
into our humanity,

and through your engrafting of your body
onto the wood of the cross.[14]   *190*
Just so,
the soul engrafted into you in truth
gives her attention
to nothing but your honor
and the salvation of souls.   *195*
She becomes faithful,
prudent,
patient.

Blush with shame, people,
blush with shame!   *200*
For by your sins
you deprive yourselves of so much good
and make yourselves deserving of so much evil!
Your good is of no use to God,
nor does your evil harm him.   *205*
Still,
he is pleased
when his creatures produce the fruit of life,[15]
so that from it
we may receive infinite profit   *210*
and eventually reach the goal
for which he created us all.

I have sinned against the Lord.
Have mercy on me!

Eternal Truth,   *215*
take those you have given me
to love with a special love:[16]
join and engraft them into yourself
so that they may bring forth the fruit of life.
I see, infinite goodness,   *220*
that just as you send the dew of supernatural light[17]
into the soul who is united with you,
giving her a calm, peaceful conscience,
so with your servants' dew

you will take away war and darkness 225
and give your bride peace and light
once again.
So do I beg you to do,
compassionate,
kind, 230
gentle God.

I have sinned against the Lord.
Have mercy on me!
Amen.

NOTES

1. Cf. *Dial.* 44, p. 90: "I showed myself to you under the figure of a tree. You could see neither its bottom nor its top. But you saw that its root was joined to the earth—and this was the divine nature joined to the earth of your humanity. . . . You know that I said to you then, 'I am your unchangeable God, and I never change. I will not draw back from any creature who wants to come to me.' " In *Dial.* 10, p. 41f., the human soul is described as "a tree made for love and living only by love." But sin makes the soul "a tree of death" (cf. *Dial.* 31–35, p. 73ff).

2. *Humanity* here is understood as the body. Cf. Gn. 2, 7: ". . . the Lord God formed a man out of the clay of the ground and blew into his nostrils the breath of life, and so the man became a living being." (Cavallini)

3. Cf. Rom. 7, 5: "When we were in the flesh, the sinful passions roused by the law worked in our members and we bore fruit for death."

4. Cf. Eph. 2, 4–5: "But God is rich in mercy; because of his great love for us he brought us to life with Christ when we were dead in sin."

5. Cf. *Dial.* 30, p. 72: "It was not enough for you to take on our humanity: you had to die as well!"

6. Cf. *Dial.* 53, p. 106: "He did not say, 'Go to the Father and drink,' but 'Come to me.' Why? Because no suffering can befall me, the Father, but my Son can suffer. And you, as long as you are pilgrim travelers in this mortal life, cannot walk without suffering, for because of sin the earth has produced thorns."

7. Cf. *Dial.* 51, p. 103: "The understanding is the most noble aspect of the soul. It is moved by affection, and it in turn nourishes affection. Affection is love's hand, and this hand fills the memory with thoughts of me and of the blessings I have given. . . . So each power lends a hand to the other, thus nourishing the soul in the life of grace."

8. Over the concept of the branches that cannot bear fruit unless joined to

the vine (Jn. 15, 4) Catherine superimposes that of the different fruits produced by the good tree and the bad (Mt. 12, 33). (Cavallini)

9. Cf. Jer. 8, 23: "Oh, that my head were a spring of water, my eyes a fountain of tears. . . ."

10. Cf. *Dial.* 17, p. 56: "But I have told you that my wrath would be softened by the tears of my servants, and I say it again: You, my servants, come into my presence laden with your prayers, your eager longing, your sorrow over their offense against me as well as their own damnation, and so you will soften my divinely just wrath."

11. Cf. Rom. 9, 2–3: ". . . there is great grief and constant pain in my heart. Indeed, I could even wish to be separated from Christ for the sake of my brothers. . . ."

12. Cf. *Life* I, x, p. 92f: "The soul which sees that it itself is nothing, and which knows that all its good is in its Creator, turns its back, with all the powers of its being, on itself and every creature, and plunges itself totally in its Creator. . . . It is like what happens when a person dives into the sea and swims underwater. He sees nothing and touches nothing but the water and whatever is submerged in the water. . . . And if the images of things outside fall in or on the water, he does not see them as they are in themselves, but only as they are or appear in the water."

13. Cf. Let. 172: "O sweet and true engrafting! For you have made us fruitful who were fruitless because we had no share in the water of grace. We have only to stretch out the wings of holy desire and lean on the tree of the most holy cross to find there this holy and sweet engrafting of the incarnate Word, God's Son."

14. Cf. Let. 27: ". . . this word made an engrafting on the wood of the cross."

15. Cf. Jn. 15, 8: "My Father has been glorified in your bearing much fruit. . . ."

16. Cf. Jn. 17, 6, 9: "I have made your name known to those you gave me. . . . For these I pray. . . ."

17. Cf. Is. 26, 19: "For your dew is a dew of light, and the land of shades gives birth."

PRAYER 18

Feast of the Annunciation, March 25, 1379.
At Rome.

On the Friday before Passion Sunday in 1379,[1] the Lenten liturgy was superseded by that of the Annunciation, and this is the theme that dominated Catherine's prayer that day.

Catherine does not often speak of Mary at great length in her writings, but what allusions there are evidence a warm and devoted regard for her. This prayer expresses that regard not only at length but with theological insight and with that poetic beauty which Catherine attains in her most exuberant moments.

PRAYER 18

O Mary!
Mary!
Temple of the Trinity!
O Mary, bearer of the fire![2]
Mary, minister of mercy!   5
Mary, seedbed of the fruit!
Mary, redemptress of the human race—
for the world was redeemed
when in the Word your own flesh suffered:
Christ   10
by his passion redeemed us;
you,
by your grief of body and spirit.

O Mary, peaceful sea!
Mary, giver of peace!   15
Mary, fertile soil!
You, Mary, are the new-sprung plant
from whom we have the fragrant blossom,
the Word, God's only-begotten Son,
for in you, fertile soil,   20
was this Word sown.
You are the soil
and you are the plant.[3]
O Mary, chariot of fire,
you bore the fire   25
hidden and veiled
under the ashes of your humanness.[4]

O Mary, vessel of humility!
In you the light of true knowledge
thrives and burns.[5]   30
By this light
you rose above yourself,[6]
and so you were pleasing to the eternal Father,

and he seized you and drew you to himself,
loving you with a special love.[7]   35
With this light
and with the fire of your charity
and with the oil of your humility
you drew his divinity
to stoop to come into you—   40
though even before that
he was drawn by the blazing fire
of his own boundless charity
to come to us.

O Mary,   45
because you had this light
you were prudent,
not foolish.[8]
Your prudence made you want to find out
from the angel   50
how what he had announced to you
could be possible.
Didn't you know
that the all-powerful God could do this?
Of course you did,   55
without any doubt!
Then why did you say,
"since I do not know man"?[9]
Not because you were lacking in faith,
but because of your deep humility,   60
and your sense of your own unworthiness.
No,
it was not because you doubted
that God could do this.
Mary,   65
was it fear that troubled you
at the angel's word?
If I ponder the matter in the light,
it doesn't seem it was fear
that troubled you,   70
even though you showed some gesture of wonder
and some agitation.[10]
What, then, were you wondering at?

At God's great goodness,
which you saw.   *75*
And you were stupefied
when you looked at yourself
and knew how unworthy you were
of such great grace.
So you were overtaken   *80*
by wonder and surprise
at the consideration of your own unworthiness
and weakness
and of God's unutterable grace.
So by your prudent questioning   *85*
you showed your deep humility.
And, as I have said,
it was not fear you felt
but wonder at God's boundless goodness and charity
toward the lowliness and smallness   *90*
of your virtue.[11]

You, O Mary,
have been made a book
in which our rule is written today.[12]
In you today   *95*
is written the eternal Father's wisdom;
in you today
our human strength and freedom are revealed.
I say that our human dignity is revealed
because if I look at you, Mary,   *100*
I see that the Holy Spirit's hand
has written the Trinity in you
by forming within you
the incarnate Word, God's only-begotten Son.
He has written for us the Father's wisdom,   *105*
which this Word is;
he has written power for us,
because he was powerful enough
to accomplish this great mystery;
and he has written for us   *110*
his own—the Holy Spirit's—mercy,
for by divine grace and mercy alone

was such a great mystery
ordained and accomplished.[13]

If I consider your own great counsel,   *115*
eternal Trinity,
I see that in your light
you saw the dignity and nobility
of the human race.
So, just as love compelled you   *120*
to draw us out of yourself,
so that same love compelled you
to buy us back
when we were lost.
In fact, you showed that you loved us   *125*
before we existed,
when you chose to draw us out of yourself
only for love.
But you have shown us greater love still
by giving us yourself,   *130*
shutting yourself up today
in the pouch of our humanity.[14]
And what more could you have given us
than to give us your very self?[15]
So you can truly ask us,   *135*
"What should I
or could I have done for you
that I have not done?"[16]

I see, then,
that whatever your wisdom saw,   *140*
in that great eternal council of yours,
as best for our salvation,
is what your mercy willed,
and what your power has today accomplished.
So in that council   *145*
your power,
your wisdom,
and your mercy

agreed on our salvation,
O eternal Trinity.   150
In that council
your great mercy chose to be merciful to your creature,
and you, eternal Trinity,
chose to fulfill your truth in us
by giving us eternal life.   155
For this you had created us,
that we might share
and be glad
in you.
But your justice disagreed with this,   160
protesting in the great council
that justice, which lasts for ever,
is just as much your hallmark
as is mercy.
Therefore,   165
since your justice leaves no evil unpunished
nor any good unrewarded,
we could not be saved—
because we could not make satisfaction to you
for our sin.   170

So what did you do?
What way did your eternal unfathomable wisdom find
to fulfill your truth
and be merciful,
and to satisfy your justice as well?   175
What remedy did you give us?
Oh, see what a fitting remedy!
You arranged to give us the Word,
your only-begotten Son.
He would take on the clay of our flesh   180
which had offended you
so that when he suffered in that humanity
your justice would be satisfied—
not by humanity's power,
but by the power of the divinity   185
united with that humanity.[17]
And so your truth was fulfilled,
and both justice and mercy were satisfied.

O Mary,
I see this Word given to you,   *190*
living in you
yet not separated from the Father—
just as the word one has in one's mind
does not leave one's heart
or become separated from it   *195*
even though that word is externalized
and communicated to others.[18]
In these things
our human dignity is revealed—
that God should have done   *200*
such and so great things
for us.

And even more:
in you, O Mary,
our human strength and freedom   *205*
are today revealed,
for after the deliberation
of such and so great a council,
the angel was sent to you
to announce to you   *210*
the mystery of the divine counsel
and to seek to know your will,
and God's Son
did not come down into your womb
until you had given your will's consent.   *215*
He waited at the door of your will
for you to open to him;
for he wanted to come into you,
but he would never have entered
unless you had opened to him,[19]   *220*
saying,
"Here I am,
God's servant;
let it be done to me
as you have said."[20]   *225*

The strength and freedom of the will
is clearly revealed, then,

for no good
nor any evil
can be done without that will.   230
Nor is there any devil
or any other creature
that can drive it to the guilt of deadly sin
without its consent.
Nor, on the other hand,   235
can it be driven to do anything good
unless it so chooses.
So the human will is free,
for nothing can drive it to evil
or to good   240
unless it so chooses.[21]
The eternal Godhead, O Mary,
was knocking at your door,
but unless you had opened that door of your will
God would not have taken flesh   245
in you.
Blush, my soul,
when you see that today
God has become your relative
in Mary.   250
Today you have been shown
that even though you were made without your help,
you will not be saved without your help.
For today God is knocking at the door of Mary's will
and waiting for her   255
to open to him.

O Mary,
my tenderest love!
In you is written the Word
from whom we have the teaching of life.   260
You are the tablet
that sets this teaching before us.
I see that this Word,
once written in you,
was never without the cross of holy desire.   265
Even as he was conceived within you,

desire to die
for the salvation of humankind
was engrafted and bound into him.
This is why he had been made flesh. 270
So it was a great cross for him
to carry for such a long time
that desire,
when he would have liked
to see it realized at once.[22] 275

To you I appeal, Mary,
and to you I offer my petition
for the dear bride of Christ your most gentle Son
and for his vicar on earth.
May he be given light 280
so that he may
with discernment
take the necessary steps
to reform holy Church.[23]
May the people be united 285
and their heart conformed with his,
so that they may never rise up against their head.
It seems to me, eternal God,
that you have made him an anvil,
for many people are striking him 290
with their tongues
and, as much as they can,
with their actions.

I pray to you also
for those you have put into my desire 295
with a special love:
set their hearts so afire
that they may be coals
not dead
but alight and ablaze 300
with charity for you
and for their neighbors.
Thus in time of need

they will have their ships well equipped
for themselves   305
as well as for others.²⁴
I am praying to you
for those you have given me,
even though I am for them
the source of continual evil   310
and of no good—
since I am for them a mirror not of virtue
but of great foolishness and carelessness.

But today I plead with you boldly
because it is the day of graces,   315
and I know, Mary,
that he can deny you nothing.
O Mary,
today the soil you are
has brought forth the savior for us.²⁵   320

I have sinned against the Lord
all my life long.
O my gentlest Father,
O boundless love!
I have sinned against the Lord.   325
Have mercy on me!

O Mary,
may you be proclaimed blessed among all women²⁶
for endless ages,
for today you have shared with us   330
your flour.²⁷
Today the Godhead
is joined and kneaded into one dough
with our humanity—
so securely   335
that this union could never be broken,

either by death
or by our thanklessness.[28]
In fact,
the Godhead was united   340
even with Christ's body in the tomb
and with his soul in limbo,
and afterwards
with both his soul and body.[29]
The relationship was so entered into   345
and sealed
that it will never be dissolved,
any more than it has been broken up to now.
Amen.

NOTES

1. The date is supplied by R. A and G supplement the basic information of date and place with mention of the prayer having been recorded as Catherine prayed in ecstasy—but this detail is probably based on a rubric in S1, where this is the first prayer in the collection. The comment, therefore, refers to the Prayers in general.

2. Cf. 2 Cor. 6, 16: "You are the temple of the living God." 1 Cor. 6, 19–20: "You must know that your body is a temple of the Holy Spirit, who is within—the Spirit you have received from God."

3. Cf. Let. 342: "Truly . . . in this sweet blessed field, Mary, this Word, engrafted into her flesh, behaved like a seed sown in the soil. With the warmth of the sun the seed springs up and brings forth flower and fruit, while its husk remains in the soil. . . . And what was this husk? It was the will of God's only-begotten Son . . . clothed in desire for the Father's honor and our salvation. So strong was this boundless desire that he ran as one in love, bearing pain and humiliation and abuse, even to the shameful death of the cross. . . . This same was in Mary, in that she was incapable of desiring anything but God's honor and the salvation of God's creatures."

4. The introductory "litany" concludes by returning to the image of the fire, of which Mary is the bearer. Again in the "chariot of fire," images of Christ and of Mary coalesce, a coalescence in itself symbolic of the close union of mother and Son. (In Let. 35 and *Dial.* 58, p. 112, the reference is to Christ; in Let. 184 it refers to Mary.) Cf. Lk. 12, 49: "I have come to light a fire on the earth." (Cavallini)

5. Cf. Let. 23, where Catherine comments on the parable of the ten bridesmaids (Mt. 25, 1–13). She sees the lamp (the vessel) as the heart. Within

is the oil of humility, which feeds the flame of knowledge of oneself and of God. (Cavallini)

6. A frequent Catherinian expression indicating the movement toward perfection, a movement which ascends from the clear knowledge of oneself and of God. (Cavallini)

7. Cf. Jer. 31, 3: "I have loved you with an everlasting love; therefore have I drawn you, having mercy on you." (Vulgate)

8. Cf. Mt. 25, 1–13.

9. Lk. 1, 34.

10. Lk. 1, 29: "She was deeply troubled by his words."

11. Lk. 1, 48: "For he has looked upon his servant in her lowliness." Also *S. Th.* III, q. 30, a. 4.

12. Our rule is none other than Christ, who in his incarnation offers himself for our reading in Mary as in a book. Cf. Let. 225: "He stands as our rule, our way, and as a book so written that everyone, no matter how ignorant or blind, can read it. The first line of this book is hatred-and-love: love for the Father's honor and hatred of sin." The image may have been inspired by the biblical image of God's writing his Law in the human heart (cf. Jer. 31, 33; Prv. 7, 1–3). Cf. also Heb. 10, 5–7: "Wherefore, on coming into the world, Jesus said . . . 'As is written of me in the book, I have come to do your will, O God.' " (Cavallini)

13. Human dignity, for Catherine, is rooted in our being fashioned in the image of the Trinity, and renewed in that image by redemption. Cf. *Dial.* 13, pp. 48–50. (Cavallini)

14. The image of a "pouch" for the human body assumed by the Word occurs already in St. Augustine, *Sermo 329, in natali martyrum:* "For he made a great exchange on the cross. There the pouch containing the price for us was split open: when his side was opened by the lance of the one who pierced him, the price for the whole world came out." (Cavallini)

15. Cf. Jn. 15, 13: "There is no greater love than this: to lay down one's life for one's friends." Eph. 5, 2: "Follow the way of love, even as Christ loved you. He gave himself for us as an offering to God."

16. Cf. Is. 5, 4: "What more was there to do for my vineyard that I had not done?" Catherine may have been recalling more directly the *Reproaches* of Good Friday (already part of the liturgy then): "What more could I have done for you? I planted you as my fairest vine, but you yielded only bitterness. . . ."

17. Cf. 2 Cor. 5, 19: "I mean that God, in Christ, was reconciling the world to himself."

18. Cf. St. Augustine, *Sermo 293:* "The sound of my voice relays the understanding of the word to you; and when the sound of my voice has relayed the understanding of the word to you, the sound itself passes away, but the word which the sound relayed is now in your heart, while it has not left my heart." (Cavallini)

19. Cf. Rv. 3, 20. Also St. Bernard, *Hom. 4,* 8–9: "Open, happy virgin, your heart to faith, your lips to proclamation, your womb to the Creator! See, the desired of all the nations is outside knocking at the door." (Cavallini)

20. Lk. 1, 38.

21. Cf. Let. 69 (XXIIII): "Know that when humankind was created by God, God said, 'Let it be done as you choose'—that is, 'I am making you free, so that you are subject to nothing except to me.'"

22. Cf. Let. 16: "This I remember the good gentle Jesus once showing one of his servants. When she saw in him the cross of desire as well as the physical cross, she asked him, 'My gentle Lord, which was the greater suffering for you . . . ?' He answered . . . 'My daughter . . . one cannot compare a finite thing and an infinite thing. Reflect, then, that my physical pain was finite, but there is no end to holy desire. . . . The cross of desire—desire to do my Father's will—began for me even as I, the incarnate Word, was sown in Mary's womb. . . . This cross was more painful to me than any suffering I ever endured physically. . . . This is why I said, 'With desire have I desired to celebrate this Passover, that is, to make a sacrifice of my body to the Father . . . for the pain of desire was driven out by the physical pain.'" Also Let 242: "God's Son . . . endured both physical torments and the pain of desire, and the cross of desire was far greater than the physical cross. . . . His hunger for our redemption, for fulfilling his eternal Father's will for him, was suffering for him until he saw it accomplished. Moreover, as the eternal Father's wisdom, he saw those who would share in his blood and those who through their own fault would not. His blood was given to all, and therefore he was grieved by the foolishness of those who would choose not to share in it. This was the crucifying desire that he bore from the beginning right up to the end."

23. Urban's zeal for reform was not always enlightened or discerning. In fact, his excesses contributed to the eruption of the schism (1378). Catherine's own policies of reform are reflected in her letters of this period. Cf. especially Let. 306, 346. (Cavallini)

24. Catherine constantly insists on the inseparability of our own good and the good of our neighbors. Cf. Let. 126: "It seems [God] wants the ship of my soul to be equipped . . . with the practice of seeking and knowing the gentle Truth, with continual groaning and prayers before God for the salvation of the whole world." Also Let. 127 (XX): ". . . since we need to equip the ship of our soul, let us proceed to equip it at that sweetest of channels, the heart and soul and body of Jesus Christ. There we shall find such an outpouring of affection that we shall easily be able to fill our souls." (Cavallini)

25. Cf. Is. 45, 8: "Let the earth open and salvation bud forth; let justice also spring up!" Ps. 85, 12–14: "Truth shall spring out of the earth, and justice shall look down from heaven. The Lord himself will give his benefits; our land shall yield its increase. Justice shall walk before him, and salvation, along the way of his steps."

26. Lk. 1, 42.

27. How interesting that Catherine should connect the image of flour with Mary's being blessed among *women!* She may be recalling the time she had made good bread from rancid flour for the poor, with Mary's help. Raymond of Capua records the incident and his own comment on it: "No wonder, then, Mother,

that those loaves tasted so sweet . . . for they were made by the shapely hands of that high and holy Queen whose sacred body was the Ark within which, so to speak, the sovereign skill of the Blessed Trinity itself kneaded that Bread which came down from heaven and gives life to all believers." (*Life,* II, xi, p. 276ff.)

28. *S. Th.* III, q. 50, a. 6.

29. *S. Th.* III, q. 50, aa. 2–3.

PRAYER 19

Passion Sunday, March 27, 1379.
At Rome.

The exact date of this prayer is a conjecture, but an almost certain one. The earliest extant manuscript, R, states only that it was recorded "in the month of March of the same year as the preceding." A and G, from what source we do not know, state simply that it was "on Sunday." Cavallini infers that it must have been March 27, and this for two reasons. First, the prayer follows that of the Annunciation (March 25) in all of the Latin collections, and is linked with it by their rubrics, so it is logical to suppose that it followed that one in chronological sequence as well. There was only one Sunday remaining in March, and that was March 27. Second, March 27 in 1379 was Passion Sunday (the second Sunday before Easter in the calendar of the day), and the theme of this prayer coincides perfectly with that liturgical context.

The prayer is a truly sublime interpretation of the Passion of Christ. In its theological depth and poetic beauty it far transcends the preoccupation with physical detail that characterizes so much of medieval writing on the subject. The Passion throughout this prayer is that "fullness of sacred time," that "acceptable time" in which human lowliness is made capable of reaching up to divine exaltedness in anticipation of eternity's vision of God "as he really is." It is the climax of the encounter of human death with the life-giving power and love of "the best of doctors."

PRAYER 19

O God eternal,
high eternal greatness!
You are great
but I am small.
This is why my lowliness   5
cannot reach up to your exaltedness
except as my affection and understanding,
together with my memory,
rise upward from my humanity's lowliness
and, in the light you have given me in your light,   10
come to know you.[1]
But if I gaze into your exaltedness,
any rising up to there
that my soul can manage
is as the dark night   15
compared with the light of the sun,
or as different as is the moonlight
from the sun's globe.[2]
For I, mortal lowliness,
cannot reach up to your immortal greatness.   20
True,
I can experience you
through love's affection,
but I cannot see you as you really are.[3]

This is why you said that we cannot see you   25
so long as we are alive.[4]
In other words,
people who are alive in their selfish sensuality and will
cannot see you in your charity's affection.[5]
If they live by reason   30
they can see you in your charity's affection,
but even so,
as long as they are living in their mortal bodies
they cannot see you as you really are.[6]
It is very true then   35

that my lowliness
cannot reach up to your exaltedness,
but can only see and experience [you]
in your mirror,[7]
and this by becoming perfect in charity.[8]   40
In this way I can see perfectly
your charity's affection—
but you as you really are?
No,
as I have said.   45

And when did I become capable
of reaching up to your charity's affection?
(Granted,
I cannot seize it as do the truly joyful
so long as I am living in my mortal body.)   50
When?
When it was time.
When the fullness of sacred time had come[9]
(which proves to be the acceptable time
when my soul realizes in your light   55
that it has indeed been announced).[10]
When the great doctor came into the world,[11]
then—
I mean your only-begotten Son.
When the bridegroom was joined with his bride—[12]   60
the divinity in the Word
with our humanity—
and the medium of this union was Mary,
who clothed you,
the eternal bridegroom,   65
in her humanity.

But this love,
this union,
were so hidden
that few knew of them.   70
This is why souls did not yet appreciate
your exaltedness.
But, as I see it,

it was in this Word's Passion
that souls came, by your light   75
to a perfect knowledge of your charity's affection.[13]
For then the fire
hidden under our ashes
began to show itself
completely and generously[14]   80
by splitting open his most holy body
on the wood of the cross.[15]
And it was to draw the soul's affection
to high things,
and to bring the mind's eye   85
to gaze into the fire,
that your eternal Word
wanted to be lifted up high.[16]
From there you have shown us love
in your blood,   90
and in your blood
you have shown us your mercy
and generosity.
In this blood
you have shown how our sin weighs you down.[17]   95
In this blood
you have washed the face of your spouse, the soul,
with whom you are joined
by the union of the divine nature
with our human nature.[18]   100
In this blood you clothed her
when she was naked,
and by your death
you restored her to life.[19]

O longed-for Passion![20]   105
But you, eternal Truth,
say it is neither desired nor loved
by those who love themselves,
but only by those who are stripped of themselves
and clothed in you,[21]   110
those who by your light
rise up in light
to know the exaltedness of your charity.

O agreeable, peaceful Passion![22]
You make the soul sail on   *115*
in tranquil peace
over the waves of the stormy sea!
O delightful, so sweet Passion!
O wealth of the soul!
O refreshment for the troubled!   *120*
O food for the famished!
O gate and paradise for the soul!
O true gladness!
O our glory and blessedness!
The soul who glories in you   *125*
discovers her fruitfulness.
And who glories in you?
Not those who have subjected the light of reason
to their sensual affection,
for they see nothing   *130*
but the earth.[23]

O Passion!
You relieve every weakness,[24]
if only the sick one wants to be healed—
for your gift   *135*
has not deprived us of liberty!
Yet more:
you, Passion, restore life
to the dead.
If the soul becomes ill   *140*
because of the devil's temptations,
you deliver her.
If she is being hounded by the world
or besieged by her own weakness,
you are a refuge for her.   *145*
For the soul has come to know in you
not only what the Word did in his Passion—
which was finite—
but she has experienced besides
the height of divine charity.   *150*
So because of you, Passion,
she wants to know and understand the truth,
to be drunk on and dissolved in God's charity

by means of your weakness—[25]
what seems to be weakness   *155*
because of our humanity which suffered in you,
but is nonetheless exaltedness and greatness
because of the mystery that came from it
by the Godhead's power.
By that power   *160*
our humanity rose up to the height of the very Godhead
and so fulfilled your purpose
in the only way it could.[26]

O Passion,
the soul who has come to rest in you is dead   *165*
so far as her sensuality is concerned,
and so she experiences your charity's affection.[27]
Oh, how exquisite and sweet
is the sweetness the soul tastes
who enters beneath this husk,[28]   *170*
where she has discovered charity's light and fire
in the sight of the wondrous union
divinity has effected with our humanity!
And she sees his humanity separated,
but not his divinity.[29]   *175*
Look, my soul,
and you will see the Word
covered in our humanity
as in a cloud.
Yet the Godhead suffers no harm   *180*
from the cloud—or rather, darkness—
of our humanity;
the divine sun and splendor
only hides there
as the serene sky sometimes hides   *185*
behind the clouds.
And what shows us this?
The fact that once the suffering was over,
the Godhead remained in the Word's body,
and after the resurrection   *190*
it made lightsome
the humanity that had before been darksome,

made immortal
what before had been mortal.

It is you then, Passion,   *195*
who point out the teaching people must follow.
So they are mistaken
who would rather follow pleasure than suffering,
even though no one can come to the Father
except through the Son,   *200*
and we cannot follow you, the Word,
without experiencing you in affection for suffering.[30]
And if the soul does not endure suffering willingly
she will have to suffer against her will.
But if she suffers willingly   *205*
by the light,
in the sun,
no weariness will overcome her—
any more than the Godhead in the Word
suffered in any way,   *210*
since his Godhead
was the willing bearer of his weariness.[31]
You clearly point out, then,
that since the acceptable time of the Word's Passion
the soul can come to know charity's affection   *215*
by the light of grace.
By this light in finite time
we arrive at a knowledge of you
as you really are
in endless time.   *220*
So it is through this lowliness of the Passion
that we come to know your exaltedness.[32]
Not that your mysteries are lowly—
they are sublime!
I say "lowly"   *225*
because it was your lowly humanity's Passion.

O gentle eternal God,
infinite sublimity!
The darkness of sin

made us unable to lift up our lowly affection   230
by the light of understanding
to your exaltedness.
So you, best of doctors,
gave us the Word
with the bait of his humanity,   235
and you caught both us and the devil,
by the power not of humanity
but of divinity.[33]
By thus making yourself small
you have made us great.   240
By being saturated with disgrace
you have filled us with blessedness.
By enduring hunger
you have sated us
with your charity's affection.   245
By stripping yourself of life
you have clothed us in grace.
By being filled with shame yourself
you have restored honor to us.
By becoming darksome in your humanity   250
you have given us back the light.
By being stretched out on the cross
you have embraced us.
For us
you have made a cavern in your open side,   255
where we might have a refuge
in the face of our enemies,
and in this cavern
we can come to know your charity
because by this you have shown   260
that you wanted to give us more
than you could give by your finite actions.
There we have found the bath
in which we have washed our soul's face clean
of the leprosy of sin.   265

O delightful love!
O fire!
O deep well of charity!

O incomprehensible exaltedness!
The more I gaze upon your exaltedness   270
in the Word's Passion,
the more my poor wretched soul is ashamed
of never having known you—
and this because I have been continually alive
to my sensuality's affection,   275
and dead to reason.
But today may your charity's exaltedness
be pleased to enlighten the eye of my understanding,
and that of those you have given me
as my children,   280
and that of every reasoning creature.

O Godhead,
my love,
I have one thing to ask of you.
When the world was lying sick   285
you sent your only-begotten Son
as doctor,
and I know you did it for love.
But now I see the world lying completely dead—
so dead that my soul faints at the sight.[34]   290
What way can there be now
to revive this dead one once more?[35]
For you, God, cannot suffer,
and you are not about to come again
to redeem the world   295
but to judge it.[36]
How then
shall this dead one be brought back to life?
I do not believe, O infinite goodness,
that you have no remedy.   300
Indeed, I proclaim it:
your love is not wanting,
nor is your power weakened,
nor is your wisdom lessened.
So you want to,   305
you can,
and you know how to

send the remedy that is needed.
I beg you then,
let it please your goodness   *310*
to show me the remedy,
and let my soul be roused to pick it up courageously.

RESPONSE:[37]
True,
your Son is not about to come again   *315*
except in majesty,
to judge,
as I have said.
But, as I see it,
you are calling your servants *christs,*[38]   *320*
and by means of them
you want to relieve the world of death
and restore it to life.
How? You want these servants of yours
to walk courageously along the Word's way,   *325*
with concern and blazing desire,
working for your honor
and the salvation of souls,
and for this
patiently enduring pain,   *330*
torments,
disgrace,
blame—
from whatever source these may come.
For these finite sufferings,   *335*
joined with their infinite desire,
you want to refresh them—
I mean, you want to listen to their prayers
and grant their desires.
But if they were merely to suffer physically,   *340*
without this desire,
it would not be enough
either for themselves or for others—
any more than the Word's Passion,
without the power of the Godhead,   *345*
would have satisfied
for the salvation of the human race.[39]

O best of remedy-givers!
Give us then these christs,
who will live in continual watching   350
and tears
and prayers
for the world's salvation.
You call them your christs
because they are conformed to your only-begotten Son.   355
Ah, eternal Father!
Grant that we may not be foolish,
blind,
or cold,
or see so darkly   360
that we do not see ourselves,
but give us the gift of knowing your will.

I have sinned, Lord.
Have mercy on me!

I thank you,   365
I thank you,
for you have granted my soul refreshment—
in the knowledge you have given me
of how I can come to know
the exaltedness of your charity   370
even while I am still in my mortal body,
and in the remedy I see you have ordained
to free the world from death.

So sleep no more,
O my wretched soul—   375
you who have slept all your life long!
O boundless love!
The physical suffering of your servants
will be powerful
because of their soul's holy desire,   380
and that desire will be powerful
because of your charity's desire.
O my wretched soul—

you who have embraced not the light
but the darkness!   385
Get up!
Get up out of the darkness!
Rouse yourself;
open the eye of your understanding
and look into the depth   390
within the deep well of divine charity.
For unless you see,
you cannot love.
The more you see,
the more you will love.   395
Once you love,
you will follow,
and you will clothe yourself in his will.[40]

I have sinned, Lord.
Have mercy on me!   400
Amen.

NOTES

1. Catherine here identifies the human person, as she often does, with the three powers of will (= affection), understanding, and memory. She returns once again, within her constant motif of self-knowledge/God-knowledge, to the interplay of the two lights, reason and faith. Cf. *Dial.* 98, p. 184f: "You know that no one can walk in the way of truth without the light of reason that you draw from me, the true Light, through the eye of your understanding. You must have as well the light of faith, which you possess as my gift from holy baptism. . . ."

2. Cf. Let. 104: "O patience, how delightful you are! . . . Your garment is a garment of sun, with the light of true knowledge of God and the warmth of divine charity. . . . This garment of yours is covered with stars—a medley of virtues. For patience cannot be present in the soul without these stars, all the virtues, together with the night, self-knowledge, whose appearance is like a sort of moonlight. And after self-knowledge comes the day, with the light and warmth of the sun. . . . It will seem to you, when you are suffering, that you are in the moonlight, but in suffering you will find the light of the sun."

3. In the dynamic of love (cf. *Dial.* 51, pp. 103–105), *affection* (It. *affetto*) is the innate tendency of the soul that moves her to love and to experience "the immeasurable goodness and uncreated love with which I created her." *Affection*

here could be that which leads the soul to experience God, or that which moved God to create. The Latin text seems to opt for the second possibility. (Cavallini) It is important to remember that for Catherine *affection* denotes the movement of the will in desire and love. It is a powerfully energetic concept for which it is difficult to find a single English equivalent.

4. Ex. 33, 18–20: "Then Moses said, 'Do let me see your glory!' He answered, 'I will make all my beauty pass before you. . . . But my face you cannot see, for no human person sees me and still lives.' "

5. Cf. Jer. 5, 21: ". . . foolish and senseless people who have eyes and see not, who have ears and hear not." Ez. 12, 2: ". . . they have eyes to see but do not see, and ears to hear but do not hear. . . ." Mt. 13, 13: "I use parables when I speak to them because they look but do not see, they listen but do not hear or understand." Also St. Thomas Aquinas, *Super Ev. S. Ioannis Lect.,* 213: "Human understanding, so long as it is conjoined with the body, cannot see God, for it is weighed down by the corruptible body and cannot attain the highest contemplation. Thus it is that the more the soul is free from the passions, and is purified from earthly desires, the more she rises upward in the contemplation of truth and experiences how sweet the Lord is. But the highest degree of contemplation is to see God as he really is; therefore, so long as we are living in the body, necessarily subject to many passions, we cannot see God as he really is."

6. Cf. *Dial.* 79, p. 149: "[They] do see me and enjoy me, though not as I really am but in loving charity and in other ways as my goodness pleases to reveal myself to you. Still, every vision the soul receives while in the mortal body is as darkness when compared with the vision the soul has when separated from the body."

7. 1 Cor. 13, 12: "Now we see indistinctly, as in a mirror; then we shall see face to face." Wis. 7, 26: "For she [wisdom] is the refulgence of eternal light, the spotless mirror of the power of God, the image of his goodness."

8. Cf. *Dial.* 167, p. 365f: "Truly this light [faith] is a sea. . . . This water is a mirror in which you, eternal Trinity, grant me knowledge; for when I look into this mirror, holding it in the hand of love, it shows me myself, as your creation, in you, and you in me through the union you have brought about of the Godhead with our humanity."

9. Cf. Gal. 4, 4: ". . . when the designated time had come, God sent forth his Son born of a woman. . . ."

10. Cf. 2 Cor. 6, 2: "For he says, 'In an acceptable time I have heard you; on a day of salvation I have helped you.' Now is the acceptable time! Now is the day of salvation!" Note that the Isaian text cited by Paul is in the context of one of the "Servant Songs," where the Servant is called to be "a light to the nations," to say "to those in darkness: Show yourselves!" (Cavallini)

11. *Dial.* 14, p. 52: ". . . when the great doctor came (my only-begotten Son) he tended that wound, drinking himself the bitter medicine you could not swallow."

12. Cf. Let. 143 (XXXVIIII): "The rational creature became a bride when God took on human nature."

13. Cf. Let. 227: ". . . in the blood of Christ crucified we come to know the

light of the supreme eternal truth of God . . . who created us for the glory and
praise of his name, so that we might experience his supreme eternal good. . . .
For if he had not in truth created us to give us eternal life . . . he would never
have given us such a redeemer. . . . So it is certainly the truth that the blood of
Christ reveals and clarifies for us this truth of his gentle will."

14. Cf. Let. 158: ". . . in his blood you will find the fire . . . and in his
open side you will find hearty love." Also P. 18: "O Mary, chariot of fire, you
bore the fire hidden and veiled under the ashes of your humanness."

15. Cf. Jn. 19, 34: "One of the soldiers opened his side with a lance." (Vulgate) Catherine, however, does not refer to an external agent; it is the fire of love
itself, smothered for too long under the ashes, that makes a way for itself to burst
uncontainably into flames. Cf. Let. 253: "O boundless tenderest charity! The
cavern of your body is opened up by the heat of the fire of love for our salvation."
(Cavallini)

16. Jn. 12, 32. Cf. *Dial.* 26, p. 65: "When my goodness saw that you could
be drawn in no other way, I sent him to be lifted onto the wood of the cross. . . .
In this way he drew everything to himself: for he proved his unspeakable love,
and the human heart is always drawn by love. He could not have shown you
greater love than by giving his life for you. You can hardly resist being drawn by
love, then, unless you foolishly refuse to be drawn." Also St. Thomas Aquinas,
Super Ev. S. Ioannis Lect., 1673: "He wanted, then, to die lifted up so that he
might raise our hearts to heavenly things. For thus he himself is our way to heav-
en. . . ."

17. Cf. *Dial.* 23, p. 60: "This love and hatred are to be found in the blood.
For my only-begotten Son gave his blood for you in death out of love for you and
hatred for sin. . . ."

18. Cf. Let. 81: ". . . the humble spotless Lamb . . . to wash his bride's
face ran to the shameful death of the cross. With the fire of his charity he
cleansed her of sin. . . . And his blood became her color, making the soul's face,
which had been all pale, ruddy."

19. Gal. 3, 27: "All of you who have been baptized into Christ have clothed
yourselves with him." Is. 53, 5: "Upon him was the chastisement that makes us
whole."

20. Lk. 22, 15. Cf. Let. 97: "O gentlest love! You were speaking of the
Passover of sacrificing your body to the Father for us. . . . You were acting like
one who has a tremendous desire to carry out a huge undertaking; when he sees
it almost finished he is joyful and glad. And with such a joy did this man in love
run to the shameful death of the cross." Cf. also P. 18, ll. 263–275.

21. Cf. Let. 98: "I am writing to you . . . wanting to see you completely
stripped of yourself so that you may find yourself perfectly clothed in Christ crucified. Consider that the more we hold back of ourselves, the less we have of
him."

22. This association of the cross with peace corresponds perfectly with the
journey over the bridge in the *Dialogue,* where the first stair is the nailed feet of
Christ, the second his open heart, and the third his mouth, "the kiss of peace."

"You know that peace is given with the mouth. So in this third stage the soul finds such a peace that there is nothing that can disturb her. She has let go of and drowned her own will, and when that will is dead there is peace and quiet." (*Dial.* 76, p. 141) Also Let. 74: "Oh, what a sight it is to see such consummate love that he has made a stairway of himself, of his body, to lift us up from the way of suffering and settle us in rest!" (Cavallini)

23. Cf. *Dial.* 31–35, pp. 72–77, for a vivid description of these "trees of death."

24. *S. Th.* III, q. 49, a. 1 ad 3m.

25. *S. Th.* III, q. 46, a. 3r.

26. *S. Th.* III, q. 48, a. 6 ad 1m.

27. Cf. *Dial.* 124, p. 238f: "My daughter, let your respite be in glorifying and praising my name. . . . And let your place of refuge be my only-begotten Son, Christ crucified. Make your home and hiding place in the cavern of his open side. There, in his humanity, you will enjoy my divinity with loving affection."

28. Catherine generally uses the image of the husk to refer to the physical human body, as in *Dial.* 78, p. 146: "The world strikes at the husk of their bodies . . . [but] the soul's orchard is closed. . . ." Here the "husk" is Christ's body, which hides his divinity. (Cavallini)

29. *S. Th.* III, q. 50, a. 3.

30. According to the *Dialogue*, they are doubly deluded who believe they can come to the Father without suffering. First, Christ is the only way, and his is a path of suffering. Second, the way of pleasure not only leads to quite another end, but is even more difficult, ultimately. Cf. *Dial.* 28, p. 68: "They are fools indeed who scorn such a good and choose instead to taste even in this life the guarantee of hell by keeping to the way beneath the bridge. For there the going is most wearisome and there is neither refreshment nor any benefit at all, because by their sinfulness they have lost me, the supreme and eternal Good." (Cavallini)

31. It is true that Catherine sees the rebellious will as the chief cause of suffering, and acceptance of what happens as a lessening of the suffering. She writes, in fact, "Your unwillingness piles weariness on weariness with your selfish will. All suffering resides in this will, for your weariness is as great as your will makes it. So, take away my will and you take away my weariness." (Let. 264) But it seems strange that she should attribute this perception, proper to human psychology, to the divinity, of its nature impassible. Perhaps Catherine's thought has been altered here by an attempt to fill in a lacuna in the text. But it can be clarified by the following from the *Dialogue* (78, p. 146): ". . . my only-begotten Son . . . was both happy and sad on the cross. He was sad as he carried the cross of his suffering body and the cross of his longing to make satisfaction for the sin of humankind. And he was happy because his divine nature joined with his human nature could not suffer and made his soul always happy by showing itself to him unveiled. This is why he was at once happy and sad, because his flesh bore the pain the Godhead could not suffer—nor even his soul, so far as the superior part of his intellect was concerned." So Catherine probably intended, in speaking

of not suffering in virtue of the will's firmness, to refer to the human soul of Christ. (Cavallini)

32. Cf. Let. 55: "O glorious blood! You give life; you have made the invisible visible for us!" Let. 227: "Once the soul has come to know the truth in the blood, she becomes drunk, experiencing God through charity's affection by the light of most holy faith."

33. Cf. *Dial.* 135, p. 278: ". . . with the bait of your humanity on the hook of my divinity I caught the devil, who could not recognize my Truth." And Let. 196 (LXIIII): ". . . when God sees how inclined to love we are, he immediately casts out the hook of love, catching our humanity to make a great peace."

34. Catherine was unusually sensitive to moral evil, even suffering physically when she perceived as a foul odor the presence of sin. Cf. *Dial.* 124, p. 238: "If you recall, when I let you smell even a bit of this stench, you were in such a state that you could stand no more, so that you said to me, 'O eternal Father, be merciful to me and to these creatures of yours! Otherwise take the soul from my body, for I do not think I can stand it anymore.' " But at this point Catherine's suffering in this regard was sharpened by the schism that was splitting the Church. (Cavallini)

35. Cf. *Dial.* 140, p. 288f, where Christ reviving the dead human race is compared with Elisha reviving the dead son of the Sunamite woman: "Member for member he joined this divine nature with yours: my power, the wisdom of my Son, the mercy of the Holy Spirit—all of me, God, the abyss of the Trinity, laid upon and united with your human nature." (Cf. 2 Kgs. 4, 8–37.)

36. Mt. 16, 27: "The Son of Man will come with his Father's glory accompanied by his angels. When he does, he will repay each person according to his or her conduct." Also Mt. 25, 31.

37. Note in left margin of R, f. 182v: "Wherever this Response occurs, it signifies that she paused, as if she was hearing something from the Lord. After listening, she would respond to God."

38. This is perhaps the only place where Catherine applies the term *christs* to the non-ordained. (Cavallini) It is, however, completely in line with the total sacramentality that emerges from all of her writings, a sacramentality that embraces every aspect of the mystery of God's union with humanity in the person of Jesus, a sacramentality that finds its most intense symbol in the blood, and that calls every believer to enter into the mystery not only as redeemed but as co-redeemer.

39. Cf. *Dial.* 3–5, pp. 28–33. Also Let. 371: "The devil . . . was not vanquished by humanity's power but by the power of the Godhead. The devil, then, neither is nor ever will be vanquished by our physical sufferings, but by the power of the fire of boundless blazing divine charity."

40. The final cry of the *Dialogue* "Clothe, clothe me with yourself, eternal Truth . . ." turns at the conclusion of the prayer away from that exhilarating "light of faith" to a climate of struggle and conflict, the painful climate of the Church wounded by schism. (Cavallini)

PRAYER 20

Thursday of Easter Week, April 14, 1379.
At Rome.

Catherine's sensitivity to the spirit of the Church's liturgy was such that her prayer again and again fed on the scriptural readings freshest in her memory. It is this fact that leads Cavallini to presume that R's dating of the present prayer on "the fifth day of April" (*5° die aprelis*) must be read as "A Thursday in April" (*feria 5ª aprelis*), and that the Thursday in question is certainly that of Easter week, when the Gospel reading in Catherine's day was the story of Mary Magdalene's meeting with the risen Lord in the garden.[1] For the theme of this entire prayer is resurrection, and its images and references are drawn consistently from the readings of Easter week, most especially that of Thursday.

The opening lines of the prayer still bask in the fire of the Easter Vigil, whose liturgy must have gripped Catherine with a particular power, given her own fondness for the symbolism of fire and water. But quickly she turns to the thoughts awakened in her by the Gospel's mention of the garden. Divinity itself is that "matchless eternal garden" which had been locked to us by our sin.[2] From this garden we had been drawn forth in creation to bear "the flower of glory and then the fruit of virtue," but sin had made us incapable of both. Only Christ, with the key of the Godhead in the hand of humanity, could open the garden to us once again, and this only by his Passion. Indeed, says Catherine, picking up on Jesus' declaration that the Messiah had to suffer so as to enter into his glory,[3] Jesus had to suffer in order to enter into his very self.

PRAYER 20

O our resurrection!
O our resurrection!⁴
O high eternal Trinity,
take my soul from my body!⁵
O our redeemer and resurrection,   5
O eternal Trinity!
O fire ever burning,
fire that never goes out,
never dims,
never can be diminished   10
even if the whole world takes fire from you!⁶
O light-giving light
in whose light we see light!⁷
In your light I see
and without it I cannot see,   15
for you are the one who is
and I am the one who is not.

In this same light of yours
I know my own need
and the need of your Church   20
and of the whole world.
And because I know in your light
I ask this of you:
that you take my soul from my body
for the whole world's salvation.⁸   25
Not that I can bear any fruit of myself,
but I can by the power of your charity,
the worker of every good.⁹
So it is
that the soul works out salvation within herself   30
and profit for her neighbors
in the deep well of your charity,
just as your Godhead,
high eternal Trinity,
worked in our humanity—   35

I mean, using our humanity as an instrument.
With a finite act
your Godhead worked an infinite profit for us
within our own humanity,
not by the power of that humanity
but by the power of your divinity. [10]   40
O eternal Trinity,
everything that has being
has clearly been created by this power,
and every spiritual and temporal power we possess   45
comes from you. [11]
It was truly your will
that we should work with these,
using our free choice. [12]

O eternal Trinity!   50
O eternal Trinity!

In your light we come to know
that you are this matchless eternal garden, [13]
and you hold enclosed within yourself
both the flowers and the fruits—   55
for you are the flower of glory,
rendering glory to yourself,
rendering the fruit to yourself,
nor can you receive this from anyone else.
If you could receive it from anyone else,   60
it would seem you would not be God,
eternal and all-powerful,
for anyone who could offer it to you
would seem not to have come from you.
But, as I have said,   65
you are both glory and fruit to yourself,
and the fruits your creatures offer you
are from you.
From you we receive them,
and therefore we can offer them back. [14]   70

We were enclosed,
O eternal Father,

within the garden of your bosom.¹⁵
You drew us out of your holy mind
like a flower   75
petaled with our soul's three powers,
and into each power
you put the whole plant,
so that they might bear fruit in your garden,
might come back to you   80
with the fruit you gave them.
And you would come back to the soul
to fill her with your blessedness.¹⁶
There the soul dwells—
like the fish in the sea   85
and the sea in the fish.¹⁷
You gave us memory
so that we might be able to hold your blessings
and so bring forth the flower of glory to your name
and the fruit of profit to ourselves.   90
You gave us understanding
to understand your truth
and your will—
your will that wants only that we be made holy—
so that we might bear first the flower of glory   95
and then the fruit of virtue.
And you gave us our will
so that we might be able to love
what our understanding has seen
and what our memory has held.¹⁸   100

And if I look at you,
O eternal Trinity,
light,
[I see that] we lost this flower of grace
by our sin,   105
and so we were neither inclined nor able
after that
to offer you glory
as you had created us to do.
So because of sin   110
you would not enter into your glory
in the way your truth had intended.

Your garden was locked up,[19]
and so we could not receive your fruits.
This is why you made the Word,   *115*
your only-begotten Son,
a gatekeeper.
You gave him the key of the Godhead,
and humanity was his hand.[20]
You joined these two   *120*
to open the gate of your grace,
because the Godhead could not open it
without the humanity that had locked it
with the sin of the first man,
nor could simple humanity open it   *125*
without the Godhead.
For a simple human act
would have been finite.
But the offense had been committed
against the infinite good,   *130*
and the punishment
had to be based directly on the sin.
So no other way would suffice.[21]

O gentle gatekeeper!
O humble Lamb!   *135*
You are the gardener,
and once you have opened the gate of the heavenly garden,
paradise,
you offer us the flowers
and the fruits   *140*
of the eternal Godhead.
And now I know for certain
that you spoke the truth
when you appeared to your two disciples
on the road   *145*
as a traveler.
You said that Christ had to suffer so,
and by the way of the cross
enter into his glory.[22]
And you showed them   *150*
that it had been foretold thus
by Moses,

Elijah,
Isaiah,
David,   *155*
and the others who had prophesied about you.[23]
You explained the Scriptures to them,
but they failed to understand
because their minds were darkened.
But you understood yourself.   *160*
What then was your glory,
O gentle loving Word?
You yourself—
and you had to suffer
in order to enter into your very self![24]   *165*
Amen.

NOTES

1. Jn. 20, 11–18.

2. Cf. the prayer for the Easter liturgy: ". . . you conquered death and opened for us the way to eternal life." (Cavallini)

3. Lk. 24, 26. The story of Jesus' appearance to the disciples on the road to Emmaus was, in Catherine's day and until the liturgical reforms of the Second Vatican Council, the Gospel reading for Monday of Easter week.

4. Jn. 11, 25: "I am the resurrection and the life."

5. Cf. *Dial.* 124, p. 238: ". . . take the soul from my body. . . ."

6. Cf. *Dial.* 110, p. 207: "If you had a burning lamp and all the world came to you for light, the light of your lamp would not be diminished by the sharing, yet each person who shared it would have the whole light."

7. Ps. 36, 10: "For with you is the fountain of life, and in your light we see light."

8. Cf. the perspective of Catherine's petitions in the *Dialogue,* 1–2, pp. 26–27.

9. Cf. *Dial.* 3–6, pp. 28–35.

10. *S. Th.* III, q. 48, a. 6r.

11. Cf. Heb. 1, 3: ". . . he sustains all things by his powerful word."

12. Cf. Gn. 2, 15: "The Lord God then took the man and settled him in the garden of Eden, to cultivate and care for it."

13. Cf. Sg. 4, 12f.: "You are an enclosed garden . . . a fountain sealed. You are a park that put forth pomegranates, with all choice fruits." The reference must certainly have been suggested to Catherine by the Gospel reading of the day, the story of Mary Magdalene's meeting with Jesus in the garden, Jn. 20, 11–18—unless the passage from the Song of Songs was in fact part of the liturgy of the day as well.

14. 1 Cor. 4, 7: "Name something you have that you have not received. If, then, you have received it, why are you boasting of it as if it were your own?" Also Is. 42, 8: "I am the Lord, this is my name; my glory I give to no other."

15. Cf. Jn. 1, 18: ". . . the only Son, ever in the Father's bosom. . . ." (Vulgate)

16. Cf. *Dial.* 51, p. 105: "It is true that when the soul decides to gather her powers with the hand of free choice in my name, all the actions that person does . . . are gathered in. . . . And then I dwell in their midst through grace."

17. Cf. *Dial.* 2, p. 27, where the image is referred to sacramental communion.

18. Cf. *Dial.* 135, p. 277: "I provided you with the gift of memory so that you might hold fast my benefits and be made a sharer in my own, the eternal Father's power. I gave you understanding so that in the wisdom of my only-begotten Son you might comprehend and know what I the eternal Father want, I who gave you graces with such burning love. I gave you a will to love, making you a sharer in the Holy Spirit's mercy, so that you might love what your understanding sees and knows."

19. Under a single image Catherine touches on three conspicuous moments in human history. From the garden of God's holy mind—creation—she carries us to the paradise of delights—the fall of Adam and Eve—and thence to the garden near the empty tomb—redemption. (Cavallini)

20. In the paschal climate that pervades this prayer, the gate of paradise is no longer guarded by the angel with the flaming sword to forbid entry (Gn. 3, 24). Now we find the Redeemer as gatekeeper, who has reopened the gate. (Cavallini)

21. Cf. *S. Th.* III, q. 1, a. 2 ad 2ᵐ.

22. Lk. 24, 13–35, the story of the disciples on the road to Emmaus, read in the liturgy of Catherine's day on Easter Monday.

23. Lk. 24, 44 (a text that is actually part of the account of an appearance of Jesus to the eleven rather than part of the story of the disciples of Emmaus).

24. *S. Th.* III, q. 54, a. 2r.

PRAYER 21

(?) August, 1379.
At Rome.

There is a gap of nearly four months between the previous prayer and the next three or four.[1] These months were, however, anything but quiet ones for Catherine.

In spite of a few significant advances within the Italian peninsula (the most outstanding being the victories of Molina and Castel Sant'Angelo), the larger cause of Pope Urban VI was faring badly at this time. For a short space in May, Queen Giovanna of Naples had, in fear for her life, proclaimed her allegiance to Urban only to retract it again. One of Catherine's disciples, Giannozzo Sacchetti, was arrested and imprisoned in Florence. Urban sent orders for Raymond of Capua to try once more to travel to France to secure the allegiance of King Charles; once again Raymond failed to go, and on May 30 Charles declared in favor of the antipope, Clement VII. Several of the Italian republics, including Siena and Florence, were lagging in their financial and military support of the Pope, causing further tensions in already strained relationships. And in each of these situations Catherine was intervening with letters. Certainly her prayers did not cease for all that, but for some reason none has come down to us from this period until this next group of three or four clustered in or around the month of August.[2]

PRAYER 21

Truth!
Truth!
And who am I
that you give me your truth?
I am the one who is not.   5
AND AFTER A LITTLE WHILE:
It is your truth then
that does
and speaks
and accomplishes   10
all things,[3]
because I am not.
It is your truth that offers truth,
and with your truth I speak the truth.[4]
Your eternal truth   15
offers the truth in different ways
to different people.[5]
Nor is your truth separate from you:
in fact, you *are* Truth.[6]
You, Godhead eternal,   20
God's Son,
came from God
to fulfill the eternal Father's truth.[7]
No one can possess truth
except from you, Truth.[8]   25
And those who want to possess your truth
must have *all* of your truth;
in no other way can they possess the truth,
which cannot be less than complete.[9]

This is how the blessed have it.   30
They see your truth perfectly,
without any incompleteness,
through their eternal vision of you,
their sharing in your vision,
the vision with which you see yourself.   35

For you yourself
are the very light by which you see yourself
and by which your creatures see you.
Nor is there anything
between you and those who see you   40
that mediates you to them.[10]
So,
as long as the blessed have a share in you,
they share in the light
and in the means by which you are seen—   45
and because you yourself
are at the same time the light,
the means,
and the very object they share in their union with you,
their vision of you   50
and their vision of your creatures in you
become one and the same vision.
And if some see more perfectly,
others less perfectly,
this is not because of any difference in you who are seen,   55
but because of the differences
among those who receive the vision.[11]

It is the same with souls in this life
who in grace receive your truth
by the light of faith.   60
By this faith
they see that the things the Church preaches to us
are true.[12]
Yet different souls,
according to their different dispositions,   65
receive this truth in different ways,
more perfectly or less.
Not that the faith is different for all this.[13]
No,
it is the same faith in everyone.[14]   70
So in the blessed,
it is one and the same vision,
though it is received more perfectly by some persons,
less by others.
Amen.   75

NOTES

1. Prayers 22 and 23 are dated August of 1379. The present prayer, though it is placed in Rome by R, carries no date in any of the extant manuscripts, yet all of these place it either immediately before or immediately after 22 and 23. This would seem to justify Cavallini's guess that its date is nearer these prayers rather than the foregoing, from which it is separated by varying numbers of prayers in the various manuscripts.

2. The date of P. 24 is also not provided by any extant manuscript, but Cavallini theorizes that it may well be dated near the other three.

3. Cf. Ps. 33, 6, 9: "By the word of the Lord the heavens were made; by the breath of his mouth all their host. . . . For he spoke, and it was made; he commanded, and it stood forth." Heb. 1, 3: "This Son is the reflection of the Father's glory, the exact representation of the Father's being, and he sustains all things by his powerful word."

4. Cf. Jn. 1, 16–17: "And of his fullness we have all received. . . . For . . . grace and truth were accomplished through Jesus Christ." (Vulgate)

5. Cf. *S. Th.* I, q. 16, a. 6.

6. Cf. *S. Th.* I, q. 16, a. 5.

7. *Dial.* 21, p. 58f: "Since they had no share in the good for which I had created them, they did not give me the return of glory they owed me, and so my truth was not fulfilled. . . . So I gave you a bridge, my Son. . . ."

8. Cf. Jas. 1, 17–18: "Every worthwhile gift, every genuine benefit comes from above, descending from the Father of the heavenly luminaries. . . . He wills to bring us to birth with a word spoken in truth. . . ." Also St. Thomas Aquinas, *De Veritate,* q. 1, aa. 4, 8.

9. Cf. *S. Th.* I, q. 58, a. 5.

10. Cf. *S. Th.* I, q. 12, a. 5.

11. Cf. *S. Th.* I, q. 12, a. 6.

12. Cf. 1 Tim. 3, 15: "God's household, the church of the living God, the pillar and bulwark of truth."

13. Cf. *S. Th.* IIa-IIae, q. 5, a. 4.

14. Cf. Eph. 4, 5–6: "There is one Lord, one faith, one baptism; one God and Father of all, who is over all, and works through all, and is in all."

PRAYER 22

Octave of the Feast of St. Dominic,
August 12, 1379.
At Rome.

Though the octave of the feast of St. Dominic is mentioned in the rubric of S1, the manuscript to which we owe the dating of this prayer, the prayer itself contains no allusion, even indirect, to St. Dominic. It is instead a meditation on the mystery of sin.

The prayer was probably in actuality a good deal longer than its recorded form, as one might infer from the rubric near its end summarizing its more personal extension and referring to Catherine's "responding to God." Her final extolling of suffering and martyrdom surely welled out of the intensity of her own deepening anguish over the state of the Church, and would find its fulfillment in just a few months.

PRAYER 22

O ungrateful people!
O high eternal Godhead,
incomprehensible, immeasurable love!

You say, eternal Father,
that those who look at themselves   5
find you within themselves.[1]
For they are created in your image.[2]
They have memory
to hold fast to you and your blessings,
and in this they share in your power.   10
They have understanding
to know you and your will,
thus sharing in the wisdom of your only-begotten Son,
our Lord Jesus Christ.
And they have a will   15
to love you,
so sharing in the Holy Spirit's mercy.
So not only did you create us
in your image and likeness,
but in a certain way   20
you bear our likeness.[3]
So you are in us
and we in you.[4]

I have not known you, God,
in myself,   25
nor have I known myself in you,
God eternal.
This is the ignorance
of the foolish people who sin against you—
for if they knew this   30
they could not help loving God.[5]
Such ignorance

comes from not having the light of grace,[6]
and this because of the cloud of sensual selfishness.[7]

The conformity between person and person is such   35
that when they do not love each other
they cut themselves off
from their own nature.

AFTER THIS SHE PRAYED FOR HER SPECIAL CHILDREN
THAT THEY MIGHT SHARE IN THE DIVINE NATURE[8]   40
BY LOVING ONE ANOTHER.
SHE RESPONDED TO GOD AND SAID:
What greater grace could I have
than to spend my life in constant suffering
and end it in martyrdom   45
for you?

NOTES

1. Cf. *Dial.* 1, p. 26: "Open your mind's eye and look within me, and you will see the dignity and beauty of my reasoning creature."

2. Gn. 1, 26–27.

3. Cf. Rom. 8, 3–4, 16: "God sent his Son in the likeness of sinful flesh . . . so that the just demands of the law might be fulfilled in us who live, not according to the flesh, but according to the spirit. . . . The Spirit himself gives witness with our spirit that we are children of God."

4. Cf. Jn. 17, 22–23: "I have given them the glory you gave me, that they may be one, as we are one—I living in them, you living in me—that their unity may be complete." Also *Dial.* 13, p. 50: "We are your image, and now by making yourself one with us you have become our image. . . . You, God, became human and we have been made divine!"

5. Cf. *Dial.* 13, p. 49: "How much greater would be your glory if you would pardon so many and give them the light of knowledge! For then they would surely all praise you, when they see that your infinite goodness has saved them. . . ." Also Let. 189 (LXXXIIII): "When the soul looks and sees in herself such a marvelously strong fire of the Holy Spirit, she becomes so drunk with love for her Creator that she completely loses herself. Though she is alive she is dead, and does not feel within herself creaturely love or pleasure, for her memory has been filled with affection for her Creator. Her understanding . . . sees and understands only her own non-being and God's goodness to her. . . . Then her love for

God becomes perfect . . . and there is no holding back the speedy course of desire; she runs on without anything binding or weighing her down."

6. Cf. *S. Th.* Ia-IIae, q. 109, a. 1.

7. Cf. Let. 2: "And if you asked me, 'What deprives me of [the light of understanding]?' I would answer, according to my lowly understanding, that only the cloud of sensual selfishness deprives us of it. . . . It deprives us of the self-knowledge from which we would learn humility . . . and it deprives us of the knowledge of God, from which we draw that sweet fire, divine charity."

8. St. Thomas Aquinas, *Opusc. Theol.* II, 1174.

PRAYER 23

August 16, 1379.
At Rome.

The mystery of sin that had haunted Catherine four days earlier (cf. P. 22) was still with her as she prayed on this day after the feast of Mary's assumption into heaven.[1] But so also was the mystery of life's ultimate triumph over the death of sin, and she prayed to be finally freed from that death through her own physical death. Her turning to Mary (l. 59) seems almost abrupt, and one senses that the Latin insertion, "And she added," must mark at least a pause in the development of the prayer. Yet the sudden dogmatic tone is not entirely unlike Catherine, who when provoked—by her own reflections or otherwise—could be quite dogmatic. It would be interesting, from an historical point of view (cf. note 19), to know just what did provoke her dogmatism in this case!

PRAYER 23

Eternal Godhead,
break the chain of my body[2]
so that I may be able to see the truth—[3]
for now my memory cannot encompass you,
nor my understanding comprehend you,   5
nor my affection love you as I ought.

O divine nature,
you raise the dead
and you alone give life.[4]
You chose to join dead human nature to yourself   10
so as to bring it back to life.[5]
O Word eternal!
You so joined mortal nature with yourself
that it became absolutely impossible
to separate it from you.   15
So on the cross
mortal nature suffered,
but divine nature gave life.[6]
This is why you were
at the same time   20
sorrowful and happy.
Not even in the tomb
could the one nature be separated from the other.[7]
O eternal Father,
you say that you clothed your Word in our nature   25
so that in him
this nature of ours
might make atonement to you for us.[8]
O unutterable mercy!
You chose to punish your own natural Son   30
for the sin of your adopted child![9]
And not only did he suffer
the pain of the cross in his body,
but the crucifying desire of his spirit as well.[10]

O eternal Father!   35
How deep and unutterable are your judgments![11]
The fool does not understand them.[12]
In fact, foolish people judge your actions
and those of your servants
by their husks,   40
not by the profound depth of your charity
or the wealth of charity
you have poured into your servants.
O ignorant, bestial people!
Why,   45
after God made you human,
have you made yourselves beasts?
And not only beasts,
but nothings!
And you judge as beasts would![13]   50
Don't you know
that bestial people are sentenced
to the eternal pains of hell?
And in those pains they turn into nothings—
not so far as existence is concerned,   55
but in respect to that grace which completes nature,[14]
and whatever is deprived of its perfection
can be called a nothing.[15]

AND SHE ADDED:
The eternal Word is given to us   60
through Mary's hands.[16]
From Mary's substance
he clothed himself in our nature
without the stain of original sin—[17]
for that conception was not a man's doing,   65
but the Holy Spirit's.[18]
The same was not true of Mary,
because she came forth from Adam's clay
by a man's doing,
not the Holy Spirit's.[19]   70
And since that whole mass was rotten and corrupt,
it was impossible to infuse her soul
into any but a corrupt material,

nor could she be truly cleansed
except by the grace of the Holy Spirit.   75
Now the body cannot receive that grace,
but only the rational or intellectual spirit.
Thus Mary could not be cleansed of that stain
except after her soul had been infused into her body—
and this was done out of reverence for the divine Word   80
who would enter that vessel.[20]
So,
just as a furnace devours a drop of water
in a split second,
so the Holy Spirit   85
devoured that stain of original sin,
for immediately after her conception
Mary was cleansed of that sin
and given great grace.
SHE ADDED: 90
You know, Lord,
that this is the truth.
Amen.

NOTES

1. The place and the day and month are provided by S1, but the year is there given as 1377. This must obviously be corrected to 1379, the only year in which Catherine spent August in Rome. R places the prayer in Rome "about the same time" as P. 25 (January 1, 1380), which precedes it in that collection. Cavallini accepts the date in S1, considering it not too far from January 1 to be reconcilable with R's designation.

2. Cf. Phil. 1, 23: "I long to be freed from this life to be with Christ, for that is the far better thing. . . ."

3. Cf. *Dial.* 82, p. 151: "The soul who has shed her body and come to me her final goal sees it clearly, and in her vision she knows the truth. Seeing me, the eternal Father, she loves; loving, she is satisfied; being satisfied, she knows the truth."

4. Cf. Jn. 5, 21, 25: "Indeed, just as the Father raises the dead and grants life, so the Son grants life to those to whom he wishes. . . . I solemnly assure you, an hour is coming, has indeed come, when the dead shall hear the voice of the Son of God, and those who have heeded it shall live."

5. Rom. 5, 17: "If death began its reign through one man because of his

offense, much more shall those who receive the overflowing grace and gift of justice live and reign through the one man, Jesus Christ." Cf. also P. 17.

6. *S. Th.* III, q. 49, a. 1; *Super I Ep. ad Thess. Lectura,* 95.

7. *S. Th.* III, q. 53, a. 4.

8. *S. Th.* III, q. 4, a. 6.

9. Cf. Gal. 4, 4–5: "God sent forth his Son born of a woman, born under
the law, to deliver from the law those who were subjected to it, so that we might
receive our status as adopted children." Rom. 8, 32: "Is it possible that he who
did not spare his own Son but handed him over for the sake of us all will not
grant us all things besides?"

10. Cf. Lk. 12, 50: "I have a baptism to receive. What anguish I feel till it
is over!" Also Let. 11: "God's Son suffered at one and the same time physical
torments and the pain of desire—and the cross of desire was greater than the
physical cross. And this was his desire: his hunger for our redemption by fulfilling his Father's command, and this was a suffering for him until he saw it com-
pleted."

11. Rom. 11, 33: "How deep are the riches and the wisdom and the knowledge of God! How inscrutable his judgments, how unsearchable his ways!"

12. Ps. 92, 7: "A senseless person knows not, nor does a fool understand
this."

13. 1 Cor. 2, 14: "The bestial person, however, does not understand the
things that are of God's Spirit." (Vulgate)

14. *S. Th.* I, q. 1, a. 8.

15. *S. Th.* Ia IIae, q. 71, a. 2.

16. Cf. the hymn *Pange Lingua:* "To us he is given, to us he is born of the
pure virgin."

17. *S. Th.* III, q. 27, a. 2.

18. Mt. 1, 20: "Joseph, son of David, have no fear about taking Mary as
your wife. It is by the Holy Spirit that she has conceived this child."

19. Gigli (whose edition was published in 1707) omitted the entire last section of this prayer from l. 59 to the end. His motive is perhaps rooted in the
controversy that had found expression in Ippolito Marracci, *Vindicatio S. Catharinae Senensis a Commentitia Revelatione eidem S. Catharinae Senensi adscripta
contra immaculatam Conceptionem Beatissimae Virginis Mariae,* Puteoli, 1663.
Marracci had proposed to demonstrate that the "revelation" contained in this last
section, concerning Mary's conception, could not be Catherinian but had to have
been invented for the sole purpose of contradicting the revelations of St. Bridget
of Sweden on the subject. Marracci attributed the "addition" to a certain Giovanni di Napoli, without, however, positively identifying that person or his work.
Marracci's argument is totally without foundation, for the section in question is
represented in the earliest manuscripts, long before the edition of 1496 in which
he claims the "addition" was made.

There is in any case no question here of revelation, but simply of Catherine's own reflections on a matter far from defined in her day. (The doctrine of
the Immaculate Conception was not proclaimed as dogma by the Roman Catholic

Church until the nineteenth century.) She is, in fact, following in this the thought of Thomas Aquinas, who held that sanctification before the infusion of soul into body was impossible, but that Mary had been sanctified, that is, freed from original sin, in her mother's womb. (Cf. *S. Th.* III, q. 27, a. 2) Cavallini accepts the authenticity of the passage. In any case, it cannot be excluded on the grounds proposed by Marracci. (Cf. Cavallini, *Orazioni,* pp. 185–187.)

20. Cf. *S. Th.* III, q. 27, a. 1.

PRAYER 24

Date and place uncertain.

Not a single extant manuscript indicates the date or place of this prayer. Cavallini theorizes that its theme of the search for truth may well relate it in time to the two prayers that are clearly dated in August of 1379. This is possibly supported by the fact that every early manuscript positions it either immediately before or immediately after these two, though the sequence of the early collections disrupts the chronology in a good number of instances. References to persecution of the Pope may be to Urban VI, but Catherine had also spoken in this vein in the *Dialogue* in reference to Gregory XI. The reference to martyrdom, however, may spring from Catherine's desire for that grace, so strongly characteristic of her last months.

Whatever the year, one is tempted to speculate that the occasion was the feast of the Triumph of the Cross, celebrated then as now on September 14. The prayer is certainly preoccupied with the mystery of the cross, and Catherine's prayer, as we have seen, very often flowed directly from the day's liturgy. Many motifs interact here: truth and ignorance, good and evil, darkness and light, the following of the cross and the persecution of it. All are bound together in the image of the Word's having engrafted himself first on the tree of humanity and then on the tree of the cross, bringing forth for us the fruit of his blood, stored now in the wine cellar of the Church.

PRAYER 24

O Godhead!
Godhead, love!
And what can I say about your truth?
You, Truth—
you tell me about the truth,   5
since I don't know how to talk about the truth.
I only know how to talk about the darkness,
because I have not followed the fruit of your cross.
I have only known and followed the darkness.
I admit that those who know the darkness   10
know the light as well,[1]
but not I—
I have followed the darkness
but I have not for all that
known it perfectly.   15
Tell, me, then, the truth about your cross
and I will listen.[2]

You say that some people persecute
the fruit of your cross.[3]
Now you yourself are the fruit of your cross—[4]   20
you, O Word, God's only-begotten Son,
who because of your boundless love for us
engrafted yourself like a fruit
onto two trees.[5]
The first was human nature,   25
so that you might reveal to us
the invisible truth of the eternal Father,[6]
the truth you yourself are.[7]
The second was the engrafting of your body
on the wood of the most holy cross,   30
and neither nails
nor anything else but your boundless love for us
held you on that tree.[8]
All this you did
to reveal the truth of the Father's will,   35

the will that wants nothing but that we be saved.
From this engrafting sprang your blood,
which by its union with the divine nature
has given us life.
By the power of this blood we are cleansed from sin[9]   40
through your sacraments,
and you have stored this blood
in the wine cellar of holy Church,
giving the keys and guardianship of it
to your chief vicar on earth.[10]   45

The only way we can know and comprehend
any of these things
is by means of your light,
the light with which you illumine the soul's noblest aspect,
our understanding.[11]   50
This light is the light of faith.
You give it to each of us Christians
when, through the sacrament of baptism,
you pour into us the light of your grace
and of faith,   55
thus washing away
the original sin we had contracted.
And we are given enough light
to lead us to our final goal of blessedness.
We have only not to blind our eyes   60
with the wickedness of sensual selfishness,
the eyes illumined by your grace in holy baptism.[12]

We blind ourselves, then,
when we put over our eyes that cloud of cold and damp,
our selfishness.   65
When we do this
we know neither you
nor any true good.
We call good evil,
and evil good.   70
And so we become ungrateful
and most ignorant.[13]
And it is worse for us to lose the light

once we have known the truth,
than before we had received the light.   75
Such false Christians are worse than unbelievers,
and the consequences are worse—[14]
except insofar as whatever little light of faith
they still have
makes it easier to accept the medicine   80
their sickness calls for.

People such as these, my Lord,
are persecutors of the fruit of your cross,
persecutors of your blood.
They do not follow you, Christ crucified,   85
but they hound you and your blood—
especially those who rebel against your cellarer
who holds the keys to the wine cellar
where your precious blood is stored
as well as the blood of all your martyrs   90
(whose blood has no strength
except by the power of your blood).[15]
They get into this rebellion
and every sort of sin
because they have lost the light of your truth,   95
the light acquired through faith in you.
This is why the philosophers,
even though they knew many truths
about your creatures,
could not be saved   100
because they did not have faith.[16]

NOTES

1. Cf. *Dial.* 42, p. 85: "For light is seen better in contrast to darkness, and darkness in contrast to light." Also Let. 211 (LXX): So you see, you mustn't be sad or run away in time of darkness, for light is born of the darkness." (Here, however, darkness does not refer to sin.)

2. Cf. Let. 216: "This gentle teacher mounted the rostrum of the cross to give us a teaching rooted in truth, and we students ought to stand down below to learn it—I mean down in the lowliness of true humility."

3. Cf. Phil. 3, 18–19: "Unfortunately, many go about in a way which

shows them to be enemies of the cross of Christ. . . . I am talking about those who are set upon the things of this world."

4. Cf. Let. 144 (XXXIIII): "O gentle and blessed Mary, you have given us the flower, the gentle Jesus. And when did this sweet flower produce its fruit? When he was engrafted onto the wood of the most holy cross."

5. Let. 27: "After the divine Word was engrafted into human nature, and the Word onto the wood of the most holy cross . . . this warm, glowing, winning love matured into the fruit of the virtues."

6. Cf. Col. 1, 15: "He is the image of the invisible God."

7. 1 Jn. 5, 6: "And it is the Spirit who testifies that Christ is truth." (Vulgate) Also Jn. 14, 6: "I am . . . the truth. . . ."

8. Cf. Jn. 10, 17–18: ". . . I lay down my life to take it up again. No one takes it from me; I lay it down freely." Also Let. 29 (XVIII): "Neither earth nor stone would have held the cross, neither nails nor cross would have held the Word, God's only-begotten Son, if love had not held him. So God's love for our souls was the stone and the nails that held him."

9. Rv. 1, 5: "Jesus Christ . . . who loves us and freed us from our sins by his own blood. . . ."

10. *Dial.* 115, p. 214: "But after I gave you my Truth . . . he suffered and died, and by his death he destroyed your death by letting his blood be a cleansing bath for you. . . . And to whom did he leave the keys to this blood? To the glorious apostle Peter and to all the others who have come or will come . . . with the very same authority. . . ."

11. *Dial.* 51, p. 103: "The understanding is the most noble aspect of the soul."

12. *Dial.* 98, p. 184f.: "You know that no one can walk in the way of truth without the light of reason that you draw from me, the true Light, through the eye of your understanding. You must have as well the light of faith, which you possess as my gift from holy baptism unless you have put it out with your sins."

13. *Dial.* 46, p. 95: "Who has deluded them? None but themselves, for they have thrown away the light of living faith, and they go about as if they were blind, groping and clutching at everything they touch. They do not see except with blind eyes . . . and so they are deceived and act like fools. . . ." Also *Dial.* 51, p. 103: "You know that every evil is grounded in selfish love of oneself. This love is a cloud that blots out the light of reason. It is in reason that the light of faith is held, and one cannot lose the one without losing the other."

14. Cf. *Dial.* 15, p. 54: "What indebtedness—to have received the treasure of the blood by which they are created anew in grace! So you see how much more they owe me after their redemption than before. . . . Because they owe me so much love . . . [f]alse Christians fare much worse [in hell] than do pagans."

15. Catherine had seen the soul of Niccolò di Tuldo, a young man she had converted before his execution, entering into the open side of Christ, "bathed in his own blood, which found its worth in the blood of God's Son!" (Let. 273—XXXI) Cf. Rv. 12, 11: "They defeated him by the blood of the Lamb and by the word of their testimony." (Cavallini)

16. Cf. *Dial.* 150, p. 316: "But alas, dearest daughter, see how those philosophers put to shame the miserable lovers of wealth who do not follow the knowledge offered them by nature to gain the supreme eternal Good! For the philosophers, knowing wealth was a hindrance to them, threw it off. But these people would make wealth a god." And Thomas Aquinas, *De Veritate,* q. 14, a. 10: ". . . for the pursuit of eternal life it is necessary to have faith concerning those things which are beyond reason."

PRAYER 25

Feast of the Circumcision of the Lord,
January 1, 1380.
At Rome.

The opening of 1380 opened also the final chapter of Catherine's life. On February 15 she would write to Raymond of Capua, in her last and farewell letter to him (Let. 373): "Father! Father and dearest son! Wondrous mysteries has God worked from the feast of the Circumcision till now—so great that my tongue could never describe them! But let's put aside that whole time, and come to Sexagesima Sunday [January 29]. . . ." Her disciple and secretary, Barduccio Canigiani, elaborates:

> The blessed maiden and mother of thousands of souls began around the feast of the Circumcision to feel such a great change, spiritually as well as physically, that she had no choice but to change her pattern of living. Eating became so loathsome for her that she could force herself to it only with the greatest difficulty. When she did, she would swallow none of it, but would regularly spit it out. Nor could she swallow even a drop of water for refreshment. From this she developed a very violent and oppressive thirst, and her throat became so inflamed that her breath seemed to be fire. But for all this, she was still in very good health, vigorous and fresh as ever.[1]

Of January 1 itself, the day Catherine prayed this prayer,[2] we know little. Aldo Manuzio tells us—from what source he does not say—that the prayer was offered at the request of a Dominican cardinal. Gigli provides the information that there were two such at the time, Fra Filipo Geza, bishop of Tivoli, and Fra Niccolò Caracciolo; and Taurisano is of the opinion that the latter is the one referred to. Perhaps it was this cardinal who had celebrated the liturgy in which Catherine had participated that day, for she prays at the end especially for "him who has given you to me today." Or perhaps it was Pope Urban himself, for she speaks of having received sacramental forgiveness that day at his hands.

PRAYER 25

O God most high!
Immeasurable love!
Fire eternal!
You illumine the human spirit.
To the extent that the soul lives in you,   5
you devour whatever she possesses that is hateful to you,
and you warm her
with the Spirit of your love.

In you I see
that the same love that drove you   10
to draw us out of yourself
with a capacity to know you
for the glory and praise of your name,
drove you besides to clothe yourself in our humanity
and to lead us back to you   15
when we had wandered away.[3]
And today for the first time,
O our lover,
you have shown us yourself as one who can suffer.
You who framed our law   20
submit yourself as one obedient to the law
to give us an example of humility.
Let us who are your creation, then,
be ashamed for being hard of heart,
for not being obedient to this law   25
while you, our God, obey it.[4]

You have shown us today the ashes of our mortality[5]
in yourself,
so that in the ashes
we may come to know ourselves in you.   30
You have shown yourself as one who can suffer,
making the down payment[6]
and stirring us up in the love of your most holy Passion,

so that after your example
we may bear our own passions willingly.[7]   35
So let every soul swoon—
no, melt—
in your love,
O my Maker and true God!
For you drew us out of yourself   40
so that from that point on we might know
and love
and follow
only you.
But we, ungrateful for your tremendous blessing,   45
have been so presumptuous
as to wander away from you,
O majesty eternal!
Today again in your mercy
you espouse our souls to you   50
with the ring of your flesh,
the ring of your charity,[8]
to be espoused to you by law
if we but recognize these blessings of yours—
by that law, I mean,   55
through which you make us sharers in your eternity.[9]

Today you have again given my soul
remission of my sins
through your vicar.
You have shown me his power,   60
which is your own.
And you have shown me that you who made us
will not save us without our cooperation.
For you who drew me out of yourself
and made me without my help   65
have not saved me today without my help.
No, you have used my plea and my confession
to free me from the bonds of my sins
through the grace of your earthly vicar.
For this   70
I your undeserving servant thank you.
And so, by your grace,
may I be cleansed.

I cry out to you today,
God eternal, my love,   75
to be merciful to this world.
Grant it the light
to recognize this vicar of yours
in purity of faith.[10]
I beg you to clothe them with this purity, my God;   80
and give him the light
so that the whole world may follow him.
And once you have given him light
beyond natural light,[11]
since you have endowed this vicar of yours   85
with a fearless heart,
let that heart be seasoned
with your holy humility.[12]
So I will never stop knocking
at the door of your kindness,   90
my love,
asking you to raise him up.[13]
Reveal your power in him, then,
so that his fearless heart
may always burn with your holy desire   95
and be seasoned with your humility.
Let him carry out his actions
with your kindness
and charity
and purity   100
and wisdom.
Thus will he draw the whole world to himself.
Give him knowledge of your truth within himself
so that he may know himself in himself—
what he used to be—   105
and you in himself—
by your grace.[14]

And enlighten those who oppose him,
who with uncircumcised heart[15]
put up resistance to the Holy Spirit[16]   110
and ward off your omnipotence
knocking at the door of their souls—[17]
for they cannot be saved without you.

Invite them,
entice them,   *115*
O boundless love,
so that they may be converted to you, my God.
Let your charity compel you
on this day of graces
to reduce their hardness to powder.   *120*
Let them be led back to you,
so they may not be lost.

And since they have offended you,
God of supreme clemency,
punish their sins in me.   *125*
Here then is my body:
I recognize that it is from you,
and to you I offer it.
Let it become an anvil for them,[18]
where their sins may be hammered out.[19]   *130*

I see that you have endowed your vicar
by nature
with a fearless heart;
so I humbly, imploringly beg you
to pour the light beyond nature   *135*
into the eye of his understanding.
For unless this light,
acquired through pure affection for virtue,
is joined with it,
a heart such as his tends to be proud.   *140*
Today again let every selfish love be cut away
from these enemies of yours
and from your vicar
and from us all,
so that we may be able to forgive these enemies   *145*
when you bend their hardness.
For them, that they may humble themselves
and obey this lord of ours,
I offer you my life
from this moment   *150*
and for whenever you wish me to lay it down

for your glory.[20]
I beg you humbly, too,
by the power of your Passion:
purge your bride   *155*
and sweep her clean of old vices
just as you have purged and swept her clean
of old barren plants.[21]
And delay no longer.

True God,   *160*
I know well that eventually you will strike
and cut off the twisted wood of your enemies' hardness
and in the end make it straight.[22]
But hurry,
O Trinity eternal!   *165*
For it is not difficult for you
to make one thing of another—
you who made everything out of nothing—
and to purge these vices.

I commend to you, too, my children.   *170*
And I present to your majesty
him who has given you to me today;
give yourself to him;
renew him today
within and without,   *175*
and direct all he does to your good pleasure.
And so that you may see fit
to listen to all these things,
I offer you thanks for them—[23]
you who are blessed for all ages.   *180*
Amen.

NOTES

1. "*Il Transito di S. Caterina*" in Taurisano, *Fioretti di S. Caterina da Siena*, 2nd ed., Roma, Ferrari, 1927, p. 179.

2. R is explicit about both date and place, and adds that the prayer was for

"the circumcision of human hardheartedness, hardened against the Church, and also for the persecutors of Pope Urban VI."

3. 1 Pt. 2, 25: "At one time you were straying like sheep, but now you have returned to the Shepherd, the Guardian of your souls." Also the parable of the Good Shepherd, Mt. 18, 12–13; Ez. 34, 11–12: "I myself will look after and tend my sheep. As a shepherd tends his flock when he finds himself among his scattered sheep, so will I tend my sheep."

4. Cf. Mt. 19, 8: ". . . for the hardness of your hearts . . ."; Mk. 16, 14: ". . . he reproved them for their disbelief and hardness of heart . . ."; Rom. 2, 5: ". . . because of your hardness and impenitent heart . . ." (Vulgate)

5. Cf. Sir. 10, 9: "Why are dust and ashes proud?" Also P. 19, where Catherine calls the humanity assumed by the Word "our ashes."

6. Cf. Let. 221: ". . . and you espoused her with your flesh. You gave your blood as a down payment, and in the end, when your body was slain, you paid the whole price."

7. Cf. Phil. 3,10: "I wish . . . to know how to share in his sufferings by being formed into the pattern of his death." 2 Cor. 12, 9–10: "And so I willingly boast of my weaknesses instead, that the power of Christ may rest upon me. Therefore I am content with weakness . . . for the sake of Christ; for when I am powerless, it is then that I am strong."

8. The Italian text has *charity*, the Latin, *flesh*. I have included both, since both have parallels in other Catherinian references to the Circumcision, e.g., Let. 143 (XXXVIIII): ". . . the fire of divine charity gave us a ring not of gold but of his most pure flesh."

9. Cf. *Dial.* 85, p. 157: "It was as if my Truth had told them: The Law is now imperfect, but with my blood I shall perfect it. . . . I will take away the fear of punishment and build it on love and holy fear."

10. To the three Italian cardinals who had become adherents of the anti-pope, Clement VII, Catherine had written (Let. 310): "I long to see you return to the true and most perfect light, and come out of the great darkness and blindness into which you have fallen. Then will you be fathers to me, and in no other way. So I call you fathers only in so far as you cut yourselves off from death and return to life . . . by being united in faith and in perfect obedience with Pope Urban VI. In such obedience live all who have the light, who by the light know the truth, and, knowing it, love it."

11. Cf. Let. 305, to Urban VI: "O my gentle shepherd, given to foolish Christians by the gentleness of God's immeasurable charity, how much you need the light, so that by the light you may recognize sin as sin and virtue as virtue, and so with discernment give everyone his or her due!"

12. Catherine recognized well Urban's need to temper his natural impetuosity in the delicate work of reform. So she wrote to him (Let. 364): "For the love of Christ crucified, temper a little those sudden impulses nature suggests to you . . . . God has given you a naturally big heart, so I beg you and I want you to try to make it big supernaturally. I mean, by zeal and desire for virtue and for the

reform of holy Church, acquire a fearless heart rooted in true humility." (Cavallini)

13. The "raising up" Catherine has in mind is the full recognition, on the part of the whole Church, of the legitimacy of Urban's claim to the papacy. (Cavallini)

14. Cf. Let. 305 to Urban: "Since it is true that you are his vicar, having been elected by the Holy Spirit and by them [the cardinals], the darkness of falsehood and heresy . . . have no power against this light. . . . This light carries with it the knife of hatred for vice and love for virtue. . . . O gentlest most holy Father . . . now is the time for you to draw this knife, to hate vice in yourself and in your subjects and in the ministers of holy Church."

15. Col. 2, 11: "You were also circumcised in him, not with the circumcision administered by hand but with Christ's circumcision which strips off the carnal body completely." Dt. 10, 16: "Circumcise your hearts, therefore, and be no longer stiff-necked." Rom. 2, 29: ". . . true circumcision is of the heart."

16. Cf. Eph. 4, 30: "Do not sadden the Holy Spirit with whom you were sealed against the day of redemption."

17. Rv. 3, 20: "Here I stand, knocking at the door. If you hear me calling and open the door, I will enter your house and have supper with you, and you with me."

18. Catherine here identifies herself with the redemptive mission of Christ, of whom she also uses the image of the anvil. Cf. *Dial.* 26, p. 65: "I made of that cross an anvil where this child of humankind could be hammered into an instrument to release humankind from death and restore it to the life of grace." Also, 155, p. 330: ". . . on the anvil of his body he hammered out your iniquities." (Cavallini)

19. There is a play on words here that is lost in the English. *Contrito,* "hammered out," comes from the same root as *contrition.* Cf. Jer. 23, 29: "Is not my word like fire, says the Lord, like a hammer shattering rocks?"

20. Cf. Let. 364, to Urban, a letter that has much in common with this prayer: "I will never rest again. . . . I want to finish my life in continual weeping, watching, and constant humble faithful prayer, for you and for holy Church."

21. These "plants" are the clergy, especially the cardinals. Cf. Let. 364: "I tell you, divine goodness is complaining that his bride has been drained by old plants, plants grown old in vice. . . . And now the new plants, those who should be vanquishing these vices with virtue, are beginning to go astray, picking up the same style. . . . You cannot in one stroke do away with people's sins . . . but you can and ought to do your duty . . . or at least what you can: purge holy Church's stomach—I mean, provide for those who surround you: sweep away the filth, and appoint people who are attentive to God's honor and your own . . . who will not allow themselves to be contaminated by flattery or bribes."

22. *Ibid.:* "Do you know what will happen if the remedy is not applied by your doing about it what you can? God wants to reform his bride completely. . . . If Your Holiness will not do it . . . he will do it himself, using great tri-

als. He will so cut these twisted branches that he will straighten them out in his own way." The figure of the "twisted branches" does not seem to appear elsewhere in Catherine's works, but that of having to "sweep out" the Church occurs also in Let. 371. (Cavallini)

23. Cf. Jn. 11, 41–43: " 'Father, I thank you for having heard me. I know that you always hear me. . . .' Having said this, he called out loudly, 'Lazarus, come out!' "

PRAYER 26

January 30, 1380.[1]
At Rome.

On the Monday after Sexagesima Sunday of 1380, January 30, Catherine began to experience "mysteries" the likes of which it seemed to her she had never before endured.

> For the pain in my heart was such [she wrote to Raymond of Capua] that my tunic was torn apart wherever I could get hold of it, while I reeled about the chapel as if I were in convulsions. Anyone who would have held me down would surely have ended my life.
>
> When Monday evening arrived I felt a compulsion to write to Christ on earth and to three cardinals, so I got someone to help me to walk into the study. After I had written to Christ on earth I was unable to write any more, so great were the worsening pains in my body. Just a little while later the devils' terrors began in such a way as to throw me into complete confusion. They seemed to be raging against me as if I, worm that I am, had been responsible for snatching from their hands what they had so long held in their possession in holy Church. The terror and physical pain were such that I wanted to run out of the study and go to the chapel—as if the study had been the source of my sufferings. So I got up, and since I couldn't walk I leaned on my son Barduccio.
>
> But all of a sudden I was thrown down, and, once down, it seemed to me as if my soul had left my body. It wasn't the same as when it really did leave,[2] for on that occasion my soul experienced the reward of the immortals and with them received the

222

same good as they. This time, though, my soul seemed like something that has been set aside, since it didn't seem to be in my body, but rather I was seeing my body as if it had been someone else. And when my soul saw my companion's grief, it wanted to know whether I had anything at all to do with that body so that I might tell him, "Don't be afraid, son"—but I could see no way to move its tongue or any other part of it except as one might move a lifeless corpse. So I let my body lie just as it was, and kept my understanding fixed on the abyss of the Trinity. My memory was filled with the thought of the needs of holy Church and of the whole Christian people. I cried out in his presence and confidently asked for divine help, offering him my desires and pressing him with the blood of the Lamb and the sufferings that had been endured. So insistent was my plea that it seemed certain he would not deny it. Then I prayed that he might fulfill his will and my own desires in all of you. After this I asked that he rescue me from eternal damnation.

I remained that way for such a very long time that the family was mourning me as dead. By now all the devils' terrors had ceased, and the humble Lamb became present to my soul. He said, "Have no doubt that I will fulfill your desires and those of my other servants. I want you to see that I am a good master. I act like the potter who smashes and refashions vessels as he pleases. I know how to smash these vessels of mine and refashion them. This is why I am taking the vessel of your body and refashioning it in the garden of holy Church in an entirely new way." And as that Truth held me close with very winning manners and words (which I pass over), my body began to breathe a bit, and it was evident that my soul had returned to its vessel. I was filled with bewilderment then, and the grief so remained in my heart that it is still there. At that point every pleasure, every refreshment, every nourishment was taken from me. And afterwards, when I was carried upstairs, the room seemed full of devils. They began to do battle with me again—the worst I have ever experienced—trying to make me believe and see that it was not I who was in my body, but some unclean spirit. I cried out pathetically for divine help, without for all that refusing the pain. Still I said, "God, come to my assistance; Lord, make haste to help me! You have allowed me to be alone in this struggle, without the comfort of

my soul's father, of whom I have been deprived because of my
ingratitude."

These storms went on for two nights and two days.[3] It was the beginning of Catherine's final and most profound exertion for the unity and
reform of the Church for whom her life had been claimed years before.

Caffarini tells us[4] that Catherine regained her ability to speak shortly after she began breathing again, while still downstairs in the chapel,
and that it was at this point that she prayed aloud what was to be the last
of her recorded prayers (other than fragments reported, whether from
memory or from notes, after her death).

The prayer, as we read it now, knowing what was to follow, seems a
most fitting overture to the three months that remained of Catherine's
life—a sort of preface to the last testament she would communicate to
her disciples bit by bit as those months unfolded. There is in it none of
the violence of the struggle that preceded and followed it, but only the
deep peace that had always seemed present at her center even in her
most anxious moments.

PRAYER 26

O God eternal,
O good master!
You made and shaped the vessel of your creature's body
from the clay of the earth.
O tenderest love!   5
Of such a lowly thing you shaped it,
and then you put within it
no less a treasure than the soul,
the soul that bears the image of you,
God eternal.[5]   10
You, good master,
my sweet love—
you are the master who breaks and refashions;
you smash this vessel
and put it back together again   15
as it pleases your goodness.[6]

To you, eternal Father,
I offer once again my life,
poor as I am,
for your dear bride.   20
As often as it pleases your goodness,
drag me out of this body
and send me back again,
each time with greater suffering than before,[7]
if only I may see the reform   25
of this dear bride, holy Church.
I beg you, God eternal:
give me this bride.

Then, too,
I commend to you my children,   30
whom I love so much.
I pray you, most high eternal Father,
if it does please your mercy and goodness

to take me out of this vessel
and not make me go back again,[8]   35
do not leave them orphans.[9]
Visit them with your grace[10]
and make them live as if they were dead,[11]
in true and most perfect light.
Bind them together   40
with the gentle chain of charity,[12]
so that they may have eager courage to die
within this dear bride.
I beg you, eternal Father,
let none of them be snatched from my hands.[13]   45

Forgive us all our sins,
and forgive me the great foolishness and neglect
of which I have been guilty in your Church—
for I have not done
what I could and should have done.   50
I have sinned against the Lord.
Have mercy on me!

I offer and commend to you my children,
whom I so love,
for they are my soul.   55
But should it please your goodness
to make me stay yet longer in this vessel,
then do you, best of doctors,
heal and care for it,
for it is all shattered.[14]   60
Give,
O give to us, eternal Father,
your gentle benediction.
Amen.

NOTES

1. The date is established in the rubric of S1 and V, which links the
prayer with Catherine's experience of the Monday night after Sexagesima Sun-

day, and states that "after that experience she was never again physically healthy but grew progressively more ill until her death."

2. She is referring to an experience, in 1370, in which she had seemed to her friends to be dead for four hours, during which time she herself was convinced that she had died. Cf. *Life* II, vi, pp. 203–206.

3. Let. 373.

4. *Libellus de Supplemento* III, i, i, pp. 276–277.

5. Gn. 2, 7.

6. Jer. 18, 3–6: "I went down to the potter's house and there he was, working at the wheel. Whenever the object of clay which he was making turned out badly in his hand, he tried again, making of the clay another object, of whatever sort he pleased. Then the word of the Lord came to me: Can I not do to you, house of Israel, as this potter has done? says the Lord. Indeed, like clay in the hand of the potter, so are you in my hand, house of Israel." Also Is. 45, 9: "Dare the clay say to its modeler, 'What are you doing?' "

7. Cf. Let. 373: "I want you to see that I am a good master. . . ." (The letter was written to Raymond of Capua on February 15, just two weeks after the event. Caffarini says Catherine wrote it with her own hand.)

8. Later in the same letter Catherine writes: "I don't know now what divine goodness would do with me . . . whether he would put an end to my miseries as well as to my excruciating desires, or whether he will in his usual way encircle my body. . . ." Here the image of the clay vessel is replaced by that of the cask held together by rings of iron. Catherine had said of an earlier experience that if God had not held her as the iron rings hold the staves of a cask, she would certainly have burst. (Cavallini)

9. Jn. 14, 18: "I will not leave you orphaned."

10. Cf. Ps. 106, 4: "Remember, me, O Lord, as you favor your people; visit me with your saving help."

11. That is, dead to selfish love, a frequent theme in Catherine's writings.

12. Cf. Jn. 17, 22–23: ". . . that they may be one, as we are one—I living in them, you living in me—that their unity may be complete."

13. Cf. Jn. 10, 27–29: "My sheep hear my voice. . . . No one shall snatch them out of my hand. My Father is greater than all, in what he has given me, and there is no snatching out of his hand. The Father and I are one."

14. Cf. Let. 373: "This body goes on living . . . with more sweet physical torments than I have ever before endured, so that my life is hanging by a hair."

EPILOGUE

Catherine's remaining months were a living out of her prayer of January 30. Only three days later the discontent of the Roman people with Urban VI rose to such a pitch that they were ready to have his life. "On the feast of Mary's Purification," she wrote to Raymond of Capua, "I wanted to hear Mass. Then all the mysteries were renewed, and God showed how great was the need, as afterward became clear. For Rome was on the verge of revolt, with base and irreverent rumors flying—but God put ointment on their hearts, and I think it will turn out well in the end."[1] The populace had besieged the Vatican, but it is reported that Urban ordered the gates to be thrown open, and awaited the mob unarmed on his throne. So abashed were they by this unexpected gesture that they declared their submission and retreated in confusion. Catherine for her part had already offered her life for the Church's peace and renewal, praying, "O eternal God, accept the sacrifice of my life within this mystic body of holy Church. I have nothing to give but what you have given me. Take my heart, then, and squeeze it out over this bride's face."[2]

As Lent approached Catherine felt herself called to be at Mass every morning, though by this time she was scarcely able to walk. Yet not only did she rise every morning to assist at Mass in her own chapel, but then, after an hour or two of rest, "you would see a dead woman walking to St. Peter's," she wrote to Raymond, "and I enter the ship of holy Church once more to work. There I stay till near the time for Vespers. I would wish never to leave that place day or night till I see this people a bit stabilized and set right with their father. This body goes on living without any food—not even a drop of water. I suffer more sweet physical torments than I have ever before endured, so that my life is hanging by a hair."

By the end of February she could push her body no more. She was half paralyzed and frightfully emaciated, yet she spent the eight weeks left her in sharing what she still could with her disciples, giving each one a direction to pursue after her death. And she suffered. And she prayed.

Barduccio Canigiani, the same who had certainly recorded many of her prayers in the months before, would later recall the last of them:

> Lord,
> you are calling me to come to you,
> and I am coming to you—
> not with any merits of my own
> but only with your mercy.
> I am begging you for this mercy
> in virtue of your Son's most sweet blood.
>> Blood!
>> Blood!
> Father,
> into your hands I surrender my soul
> and my spirit.[3]

It was April 29, 1380, and she was thirty-three years old.

NOTES

1. Let. 373.

2. Let. 371 (which Caffarini says is a companion to 373, addressed also to Raymond, though Tomasseo marks it as having been written to Urban VI; Caffarini is almost certainly right).

3. Letter to Sister Catherine Petriboni of the monastery of San Piero a Monticelli, in *Lettere,* ed. Tommaseo-Misciattelli, 1940, vol. VI, pp. 143–153.

Appendix I: TEXTUAL NOTES

These notes are provided for those whose use of the *Prayers* requires a knowledge of any variations among the texts on which the translation is based, and of any departure from an exact rendering of the text as it stands. I have placed them here, however, to keep them from being a distraction from the *Prayers* themselves.

Unless these notes indicate otherwise, I have basically followed the Italian text as established by Giuliana Cavallini. Variants from this are indicated here by line of the translation. The codices in which the variants occur are cited by their symbols as given in the Introduction; *L* refers to all of the Latin codices, and *It* to all of the Italian. When entire lines vary significantly, I have simply given the entire substitution. When it is a question of only a word or so, the variant is given first, and then, after a slash, the matter it replaces (e.g., *infinite / great* = "*infinite* instead of *great*"). Matter omitted in a codex is indicated by square brackets.

I have included here only those variants which affect the content and meaning of the text. I have not, therefore, noted spelling variations, obvious copyist errors, or differences of structure only. In the few instances where it has seemed advisable to be somewhat free in the interest of clarity, I have given the literal translation (*Lit.*) in these notes.

Prayer 1

7	S2: [*as . . . creatures*].
11	It: [*in this*].
13	It, N: [*very*].
14	L: [*Godhead eternal*].
15–19	L: *You gave us memory fashioned after you, eternal Father, to hold and keep what the understanding sees and comprehends of you just as you keep all things within yourself.*
20	It: *And so.*
21	S2, V: *we share through our understanding in the wisdom.*

23	L: *You also gave humankind the will of the Holy Spirit.*
28–30	The final clause in It is: *Thus, with the will and strong hand of love, our memory and affection are filled with you.* L has simply: *and fills our memory and affection with you.* I have combined elements from both.
31	L: [*high eternal Godhead*].
32	L: *this world/us;* but R is corrected to match It.
32	L: *infinite/great.*
34	L: *giving us understanding to know you.*
35	L: [*to keep you in mind*].
38–40	L: *as is reasonable.*
45	L: *their Maker/you.*
46	L adds *whose very life is always in you.*
47	L: *goodness/Godhead.*
48	L: [*ineffable love*].
49–51	S2, V: [*in you. . . wretches*].
56	L, S2, V: [*high eternal Father*].
57	L: [*only-begotten*].
60	L adds *true God and Lord.*
62	L: *fashioner/refashioner.*
65	L: *the Father's/our.*
66	L: *our Creator/God.*
68	L: *most holy body/body.*
70	L: *by being made obedient.*
72–77	L: [*On the cross . . . that*].
77	L: *making/made.*
80	The text, in almost every place where this invocation occurs, has *domino,* influenced perhaps by the text of 2 Sm. 12, 13: "*Peccavi domino*" ("I have sinned against the Lord").
83	L: *I find incomprehensible love from you, good Jesus, my God, for the creature fashioned after yourself.*
85	L: [*alone*]
85–88	N: [*for it is you . . . exist*].
86	S2, V: [*and human*].
89	L adds *capable of holding your knowledge and infinite power and goodness.*
96	L adds (*as we are bound to*).
97	S2, V add *to love;* L: *we see in you your priceless Godhead.*
98–99	L: *you are a man of ineffable purity;* S2, V: *ineffable/priceless.*
101–03	L: *And if we want to direct our zeal to God, you shed your own blood as the priceless price of our redemption.*
102	S1: [*you are Lord*].
103	S2: [*the price*].
110	S2, V: *salvation/wretchedness.*
105–33	L: *you, therefore, are Lord. You were our father, brother, teacher,*

friend, and companion when in your boundless kindness and charity you kept company with us. O eternal Godhead, what thanks can I, wretched creature, give you for these things—you who live in highest wisdom and infinite power and goodness? You are purest beauty; I am the vilest of creatures. I am death; you are everlasting life. You are light; I am darkness. You are wisdom; I am ignorance. You are infinite; I am frailty coming every day nearer my end. You are the doctor; I am a sick weak sinner who, because I fritter away myself and my time uselessly away from you, am never found loving you who have drawn us to yourself and keep drawing us back to yourself by grace if we only let you and if our will does not rebel against your most holy majesty.

113–25   S2, V: *I am the vilest foolishness. You are supreme eternal goodness and I a wretched creature. You are life and I am death; you light and I darkness; you wisdom and I ignorance; you infinite and I finite; you the doctor and I a sick weak sinner who have never loved you.*

144   S2, V: [*supreme*].

148   R has this line written in the margin.

152–53   It: *our life and our death rest in him to the extent that he is careful.* (I have followed the more consistent Latin here.)

164   L adds *God.*

166   L adds *from you.*

168–69   S2, V: *with my flesh and blood.*

176   L: *humbly beg/beg.*

180   S2, V: *Give him a new heart;* L: *Give him, God, a new heart.*

181   L; *your grace/grace.*

183   L: *faithful/unbelievers.*

184   L: *in the saving fruit of the passion and poured-out blood.*

187   L: [*high . . . Godhead*].

188   L adds *eternal Godhead.*

189   S1, N add *Amen.*

Prayer 2

1–2   L: [*Godhead! Godhead!*].

4   L: [*and do not deny*].

6   L: *in which the soul feeds like a fish on you yourself.*

9   L: *most high/high.*

15   L: [*O . . . love*].

16   L: [*you are showing*].

19   L adds *and that of sinful creatures.*

21   L: [*This . . . will*]; S2: [*that . . . will*].

27–28   L: *which tests and judges between you and themselves according to your will, as fire tests your gold, motivated only by love.*

34–35   L: *But I, wretch, by loving sin have constantly wasted the time of divine obedience.*

41   S2 adds *Lord.*

42	L: [*great many*].
43	S2, V: add *my Lord.*
44	L: *holy mother Church/holy Church.*
46	L: *fattened (saginatum)/slain.*
49	L: *in your heavenly way, not their own death-bound way.*
	N: *not the death-bound way of the godless.*
52	S2, V add *O eternal Father;* L: *confect and administer/administer.*
54–55	L: *Let them not be like beasts who have no reason and are unworthy of this.*
55	S2, V: [*have . . . and*].
57	S2, V: *consume/wash.*
57	L adds *author of peace.*
60–61	L: *losing the useful time they have for the useless time they do not have.*
72	L: *ineffable true God* (R: *ineffably true God)/ineffable Godhead.*
73	S2, V: [*Amen*].

Prayers 1 and 2, Abridged Version

30	S2: [*and refashioner*].
48	V: *and I am frail and sick.*
62	V: *supreme clemency/clemency.*
115	S2: *goodness/will.*
134	V: *ministers of your bride, holy Church/your holy bride's ministers.*

Prayer 3

35	It: *your/his.*
40	It: [*same*].
71	N (in margin): *charity/compassion.*
75	L: *win/buy back.*
91–92	This is one of the few instances that the invocation is in the vernacular in the Italian text.
113	L: *follow/do.*
117	A: *and because divine things are lacking except in you.*
128	It: *power/penance.*
130	Lit: *You came to us with abuses.*
142	Italian *essa* (f.) could refer only to *goodness,* which does not fit the context. I have therefore followed the Latin.
142	Lit: *. . . cleanse our weakness.*

Prayer 4

4	Sa: *IN HER LOVE/AS WAS HER CUSTOM* (*amore/more*).
10	L: *as I liken you.*
29	Lit: *best* (It: *ottimo;* L: *optime*)
63–71	L omits

Prayer 6

1	S2, V: [*O*].
2	S2, V: *and by your power draw it to yourself.*
5–6	S2, V: *and warm me with your most holy love.*
7	S2, V omit.
8	S3 omits.
10	S2, V omit; A, G add *Amen.*

Prayer 7

9	R: [*light of*].
13	L adds *our Lord;* R: *And you have made our Lord Jesus Christ.*
28	It: [*your*].
45	L: *holy mother Church/holy Church.*
55	N: *holy faith/faith.*
86	Lit: *newly inserted things.* Perhaps *inserite* (L: *inserta*) is a mishearing of *innesti* ("engraftings"), an image frequently used by Catherine. I have, with Cavallini, followed that assumption, as it fits the context.
95	Again I have followed the Latin as more consistent. It: *let them be engrafted in these new virtues.*
98	N: *virtuous and fruitful works;* R: *virtuous/fruitful.*
105	It: *May he serve in the presence of your grace.*
115	G: [*Amen*].

Prayer 8

16	L: *desires/desire.*
19	It: [*into . . . peace*].
54	R: *all/as we pray.*
58	L: *this/your.*

Prayer 9

22	L: [*along . . . paths*].
27	L: *everyone's will/all things.*
29–30	L omits.
60	L omits.
61	It: *understood and received/learned . . . heart.*
69	L adds *to the Father.*
70	Lit: *I know not how to see any other road.*
75	L: *precious blood/blood.*
83	L adds *and deep well of charity.*
86	L omits.
96	Lit: *founded with your blood.*
104	L: [*more surely*].
108	L omits.
111	L: *worthily say/say.*

112	*justly and truly make/make.*
113	L: *Surely we shall say and shall believe with a sure judgment.*
114	L: [*gentle*].
122	L: *We your creatures/We.*
125	A, G: *side/mud.*
126	L: *Truth/Godhead.*
129	L: *human servants/servants.*
133	L: *your mercy/the same mercy.*
134	L, except R: *The same/Your;* R: *Your mercy shields us.*
137	L: *unclean animals/animals.*
141	L: *rules/preserves.*
142	L: *and puts off our death.*
148	L: *mercy alone/mercy.*
153	L omits.
155	L: *crown/reward; rightly/bravely.*
156	L: [*with . . . patience*].
162	L: *how we neither can nor may in any way.*
166	L adds *poor as I am.*
172	It: [*complete*].
180	L: *, collectively, sinned/sinned.*
182	L: *Secondly and lastly.*
192	L omits.
201	L: *with spiritual as well as physical pain.*
206–08	It omits.

Prayer 10

4	L: *truly madly/madly.*
9	It omits.
14	L: [*wisdom*].
17	L: *what have you ever received from humankind but offense?*
21	L omits.
30	L: *this/you.*
42	L: *as food, the whole Trinity.*
44–45	L: *Certainly nothing but your charity!*
46	L adds *O eternal Trinity.*
56–57	R omits.
58	L adds *only for yourself.*
64	Lit: *So we see that to such as these. . . .*
64	L: *reveal/give.*
66	R: *people's/the devil's.*
68	L omits.
69–70	L: *against every sort of difficulty.*
72	L: *light/truth.*
73	L omits.
75	L: *with your mercy, the Holy Spirit.*

77	It omits.
79	L: *which each one brings to you.*
81	L: *each has used his or her life.*
87	L: [*bride, holy*].
89	L: *And I humbly beg you.*
91	L: *truth/need.*
93	L: *creatures/ministers.*
104	L: *in the fire of his love.*
105	L: *O eternal Father.*
112	L: [*the reform of*].
129	Lit: *your creature that has reason;* L has simply *creature.*
131	A, G: [*new*] (*creazione* instead of *recreazione*).
131–32	L omits.
135	L: [*and generous.*].
136	L: *part/goodness.*
139–40	L omits.
142	L: [*constant*].
146	L: *constant dwelling/dwelling.*
150–51	L: *that you have not grounded your heart the least bit in virtue.*
163	L: [*absolute*].
164	L: [*terrible*].
171	L: *as you have deigned to give.*
189	L: [*against them*].
191	It: [*to you*].
199	A, G: *Let it be your will that I see.*
199–202	L: *But I want to see in your creatures that they give you glory as they should, by reaching. . . .*
202	L: *everyone/them.*
210	L adds *I humbly beg.*
213	S1: [*Amen*].

Prayer 11

7	Lit: *the source of light is known.*
9	L: [*all*].
10	L: *we creatures/we.*
12	Lit: *what light does in the soul is known.*
25	L: *darkness of this mortal life/dark.*
32	L: *any creature/the soul.*
69	L adds *O boundless love.*
73	L: *but all these things at your good pleasure.*
75	L: *It can truly be called a sun.*
87	L adds after this line: *Such a soul is made strong in your power, eternal Father, and prudent in the wisdom of your only-begotten Son, and ready to love, sharing in the Holy Spirit's mercy.*
108	L adds: *Wherever I turn the eye of my understanding.*

149	L adds *in your light.*
153	L: *and she has seen in this same light of yours that this free love.*
161	L: *has gotten or might get/might get.*
168	R: *actual light/light of understanding.*
187	L: *You, supreme wisdom.*
190	L: *You who are eternal strength.*
209	L: *from such conformity/from you.*
267	L adds: *You want everyone to take off this garment at once and completely, ripping it off in a single pull.*
282	L: *you, high eternal Godhead/you.*
286	L: *[and love].*
308	L omits.
310	L: *and you are the only one who is.*
317	L: *vicar on earth/vicar.*
323	L omits.

Prayer 12

14	L: *eternal and immeasurable/eternal.*
15	L: *In what place did you deign to come down to give us yourself?*
33	L: *weakness/baseness.*
44	L: *my own will/myself.*
62	L: *the least of them out of love/them.*
63	L adds *because you are all-powerful.*
156	L: *without eating or wanting to eat this food of souls.*
158	L: *Infinite goodness.*
174	L: *Enlighten also, most merciful Father.*
189	L: *love them/love.*
198	L omits.
199	L: *So the word of Paul is well verified.*
206	L: *who alone are all good.*
221	L: *your/my.*
235–36	L: *to cut yourselves off from your noble nature by committing sin?*
237	The Latin text here inserts the following: *O sweet eternal Godhead! The other things we see that do not have the appearance of fire—how are these fire? Response: I see that all things are fire because, as has been said, you created all things out of love. For example, a plant, so long as it remains in the earth, though it is not earth, none the less receives its substance from the earth. So it is indeed true that nothing is anything but fire.* Cavallini comments: "The insertion in the Latin text . . . sounds entirely like an addition, dictated probably by a desire to rectify the contrast between the affirmation that human nature shares in the divine fire (that is, charity), and the fact that the human person acts against charity by sinning. Thus the question: how can what does not act like fire be fire? But the response, in spite of a certain assonance with other Catherinian passages

(cf. P. 18: 'You are the soil, and you are the plant'), does not sound persuasively like an expression of Catherine's thought, which is always clothed in perfectly appropriate images. How could she have thought to identify the divine nature with earth—and precisely at the end of a prayer in which the constantly recurring theme is that of God as fire of charity? Earth is an image Catherine generally uses to refer to human nature and its passions, or self-knowledge, but it is never referred to God." (*Le Orazioni*, pp. 259–261, n. 26)

239	L: *You, true light.*
249	L: *upright/free.*

Prayer 13

8	N: [*and blood*]; L: *your beloved/your.*
9–10	L: *wherein you give me your whole self, God and man.*
18	L adds *boundless love.*
22	S1, R: *your creature's beauty;* N: *your creature's love/your creature.*
34	It: *we;* S1, R: *all of us/I.*
51	L has *In this Word* at the head of the next sentence.
55	L: *in the very great shedding of his blood.*
60	S1: *when you opened the ear of the Godhead (aperuisti aurem/operuisti amum).*
64	L: [*love and*].
71	L: *your creature has/we have.*
75	L: [*mind's*].
78	L: [*blind*].
101	L: *most merciful Father.*
104	L: *all;* It: *your creatures* (I have used both for clarity).
111	L: *ask and you shall receive.*
113	L: *I, most wretched one/I.*
114	L: [*seeking and*].
117	L: [*whole*].
118	N: *mother Church/Church.*
121	L: [*my love*].
125	L: *the Lord God/God.*
130	L: *his/your Creator's.*
139	L: *your creatures/us.*
166	L: *for your Son, the Word.*
186	L: *O unutterable eternal love.*
215	L omits.
224	L omits.
232	L: *Grant, I beg/Grant.* S1, N: *merciful;* R: *holy/gracious.*

Prayer 14

7	L: *your most sweet/your.*
9	*what/who.*

10	L: *from following it up with the effect of good works?*
24	L: *in the presence of your majesty.*
34–41	L: *You also foresaw within yourself a suitable help, namely, preserving the wounds in his body.*
43	L: *lay in reconciling us creatures to yourself the Creator.*
45–46	L: *so also you saw this.*
47	L: *I have seen and known/I know.*
49	L: *in and with/in.*
54	L: *holy mother Church's need.*
59	L adds *your bride.*
65	L: *of mine and of every rational creature/in us;* N has only *of mine.*
66	L: *to forget and rebel/to rebel.*
68	L: *[often].*
70	L: *knew/saw.*
85	L: *will/strength.*
91	L: *insuperable/eternal.*
101	L: *in the likeness of/out of.*
113	L: *So/One thing.*
114	L adds *put into the hand of free choice.*
118	Here I follow the Latin, which has *homo* as the subject of this clause and the next, where the Italian keeps *the will* (which cannot know) as subject.
126	L: *So it is clear that/So.*
138	L: *that nourish the fire in the soul and make it grow.*
143	It: *your/the* (it is, however, *faith* that is being addressed, not God).
152	L: *supreme peace/tranquility.*
170	The Latin text only has here a recapitulation of what has preceded. I give it here rather than in the text of the prayer itself, since it is wholly repetitious. There is no clear reason, though, to conclude that it was not in the original prayer as recorded, for such recapitulation is characteristic of Catherine's style. The insert: *In your light you have shown me that you foresaw the sin humankind would commit, and the remedy for that sin, the redemption you accomplished afterward through the Word. [You have shown me] that you foresaw our human weakness and a help for that, namely, the wonder of the will given us by you, supreme exaltedness. But what is it that guides and nourishes this will? The light of most holy faith. This light is the chief means and the end of every sort of perfection; it is this very light that preserves and increases perfection in the soul. This light perfects charity within itself, and is itself preserved and increased by charity, as I have said.*
192	L: *holy mother Church/holy Church.*
207	L: *[you require of him].*
220	N: *can/must.*
221–22	L: *for the salvation of the whole world and the reform of your Church.*
224	L: *I have sinned, I have sinned, Lord!*

| 229 | L: [*I have received from you*]. |
| 230 | R, S1: *I acknowledge, eternal God, that your goodness;* N: *eternal goodness/goodness.* |

Prayer 15

3	L adds *I beg.*
12	L: *For I see that/For.*
13	L: [*to death*].
59	L: *according to that saying.*
74	L: *each person's/our.*
79	L: *see/know.*
80	L: *see/know.*
84	L: *Be compassionate and have mercy on us.*
97	L: *the world/us.*
99	L: *the greatest/even greater.*
107	L: *and calm the anger of your indignation.*
139	L: [*that is yourself*].
143	L: *within the soul as you enlighten her?*
166	L: [*good*].
176	L: *laying her body open to death.*
181	L: [*your mysteries*].
195	L: *mortal sin/sin.*
197	L omits.
202	Lit: *body.*
218	L: [*only-begotten*].
223	L: *shadow of your wings/wings of your mercy.*
224	L: *so that the wickedness of the proud.*
228	L: [*and scatter*].
229	L: *this your garden/this garden.*
242	It: *con tutto l'affetto;* L: *toto cordis affectu.*
248	L: *us great wretches/your creatures.*
250	L: *the hardness of our heart/the human heart.*
256	R: *slave or enemy/slave.*
265	It: *fruit in you/fruit of life* (I have followed the Latin here as more consistent with the context).
275	L: *I insist, O eternal God.*
283	L: *finite and very brief/finite.*
290	L: *Certainly the same compassion.*
307	L omits.
321	L: [*it . . . difficult*].
351–53	L: *you let the just experience spiritual peace and calm in this life.*
360	L: [*justice and*].
368–70	L: [*In . . . time*]; It: [*I have not known you, and so*]. The inclusion of the reference to knowledge seems to flow from the preceding sentences, so I have combined both texts.

371	L: *I commend to you most closely (strictissime) my children.*
374	It: [*You commissioned me*]; again the Latin seems more complete.

Prayer 16

1–2	N omits.
5	N omits.
12	Lit. *father* where I have *parents* throughout this sentence. The plural, however, is consistent with Catherine's description of original sin, *Dial.* 14, p. 51.
34	L: *cereum (impressionable, like wax)/ready.* The translator may have had in mind Catherine's image elsewhere of the soul as warm wax that holds the imprint of a seal. However, the latter is a positive image: of grace remaining in the soul after sacramental communion (*Dial.* 112, p. 211), or of the imprint of the Holy Spirit's salvific love and desire in the humanity of Jesus (Let. 30 [I]). In all other instances in this prayer the Latin has *aptus (ready)*. (Cavallini)
68	It: *the pleasures and wretched things of the world;* L: *the wicked things of the world.*
107–11	L: *as long as holy desire stands firm and grows, for if at some time desire should become lukewarm and lax, rebelliousness would at once be roused more alive than before.*
130ff	G omits this postscript entirely. L: *Then in her usual way our mother prayed for God's Church, for Christ's vicar, and for her children, and for all people. Amen.*

Prayer 17

1	N: *Blessed Trinity!*
22	L: *What fruit does the memory produce?*
30	L: *fashioned/planted.*
31	L adds *eternal God.*
84	It: *Besides, we must engraft ourselves into and conform ourselves to you.* (I have followed the Latin, which is more logical.)
85	It: *through the way of suffering and holy anguished desires.*
88	N: *if we choose to remain in you.*
89–91	L omits.
151	L: *O my love, what light.*
159	L adds: *We must follow him, not you the Father, because, as has been said, no suffering was or could be in you.*
178	L omits.
180	L: [*the fire of*].
185	L: *most holy cross/cross.*
189	L: *consecrated body/body.*
196	L: *She becomes wise, faithful.*
207	L: *Supreme goodness is pleased.*

226	L: *most gentle bride/bride.*
228	L: *So do I humbly beg you to do.*
229–31	L omits.

Prayer 18

9	L: *Christ/the Word.*
27	L: *Under your ashes, which ashes are our humanness.*
30	It: *lives/thrives.*
39	L: *humility/divinity.*
42	L: *moved and drawn/drawn.*
44	L: [*to us*].
55	L: *believed/did.*
64	Lit: *that this was possible with God.*
68	L: *light of God/light.*
74	L: *Certainly at God's great goodness.*
79	L: *of receiving such great grace.*
84	L: *great and unutterable/unutterable.*
88	R adds *I mean slavish fear.*
89–91	L: *but wonder at God's boundless goodness in the face of the small-ness—indeed the all but nothingness—of your virtue.*
102	L: *whole Trinity/Trinity.*
109	L: [*great mystery*] (the Latin frequently omits or changes Catherine's usage of *mystery*).
111	N: *the mercy of himself, the Holy Spirit of the Father.*
113	N: *ministry.*
124	L: *sold and lost/lost.*
141	It: [*of yours*].
145–49	L omits.
152	L: *chose for our salvation/chose.*
154	L adds *by saving us and.*
157	L: *that we might perfectly share.*
158	L: *and be fully glad.*
164	L: *as is having mercy and sparing.*
169	L adds *of ourselves; to your justice/to you.*
171	It omits.
172	It: *you, eternal Trinity/your eternal unfathomable wisdom.*
239–41	L omits.
248	N: [*today*].
249–50	L: *God has contracted and effected a relationship with Mary.*
254	Text prefixes *So, as has been said.*
262	L: *in which this teaching is written out and set before us.*
263	L: *I see that this wisdom, that is, the only-begotten Word of God.*
278	L: *Son our Savior/Son.*
285–86	It: *May the people be united, and the people's heart be conformed to his.*

290	It: *everyone/many people.*
295–96	L: *for the most beloved children given me by you.*
297	L: *them/their hearts.*
300	L: [*alight and*].
304	L: *they will have the ships of their souls secured and well-equipped.*
313	N: *impatience/carelessness.*
317	It: *that nothing is denied you.*
323–24	It: *O gentlest boundless love!*
328	It: [*proclaimed*].
343	It omits *afterwards,* which in the Latin makes it clear that Catherine has in mind the risen Christ.
349	L omits.

Prayer 19

5	S1: *weakness/lowliness.*
9	S1: *weakness/lowliness.*
11	L: *I come to know you.*
41	L translates It *perché* as *quia* (because).
42	It: *effect/affection.*
361	L: *that we see nothing but ourselves.*
363	L: *I have sinned against the Lord.*
390	L: [*into the depth*].
399	L: *I have sinned against the Lord.*

Prayer 20

44	Lit: *is seen to have been created by this power.*
164–65	L: *Did you have to suffer in order to enter into yourself?*

Prayer 21

6	It omits.
23	L: *will/truth.*
25	L: [*Truth*].
29	Lit: *which can suffer no incompleteness.*
37–38	L: *are the very light by which your creatures see you.*
74	It adds *as has been said.*

Prayer 22

39	It: *this blessed virgin/she;* L: [*children*]
42–46	It omits.

Prayer 23

10	A: *mortal/dead.*
30	R: [*natural*].
56	It: *nature's being/nature.*
59–93	G omits (cf. note 19).

59	It omits.
71	L: [*and corrupt*].
73	L: *rotten nature/corrupt material.*
80–81	L: *and this was done out of reverence for the divine treasure that would be put into that vessel.*
90	It omits.
93	R omits.

Prayer 24

16	L: *Tell me, then, Lord/Tell me, then.*
64	L: *those cataracts/that cloud.*
71–72	L: *And so we become most ungrateful and more than most ungrateful.*
87	L: *vicar/cellarer.*

Prayer 25

49	L: *also/again.*
53	L: [*by law*].
57	L: *also/again.*
63	Lit: *will not save us without us.*
65	Lit: *and made me without me.*
66	Lit: *have not saved me today without me.*
69	It: *through the grace of your earthly vicar.*
120	L: *soften/grind.*
148	R: *spare/obey.*

Prayer 26

16	L: *most generous goodness/goodness.*
23	L: *call/send.*
39	L: *in your most perfect light.*
49	L adds *conscientiously.*
50	L: *all that/what.*
51	L: *I have sinned, Lord!*

Appendix II:
INDEX OF BIBLICAL ALLUSIONS
NOTED

SELECTED BIBLIOGRAPHY

(For Manuscript data, see Introduction.)

Catherine of Siena (Caterina da Siena). *Epistole Devotissime de Sancta Catharina da Siena (e Orazioni)*. Edited by Aldo Manuzio. Venetiis: Aldus Manutius, 1500.

————*L'Opere della Serafica Santa Caterina da Siena Nuovamente Pubblicate da Girolamo Gigli*, Vol. IV, *Il Dialogo e Le Orazioni*. Siena: Bonetti, 1707.

————. *Le Orazioni*. A cura di Giuliana Cavallini. Roma: Edizioni Cateriniane, 1978.

————. *Preghiere ed Elevazioni*. A cura del P. Innocenzo Taurisano. Roma: Ferrari, 1920.

————. *Tutte le Preghiere ed Elevazioni di S. Caterina, Dottore della Chiesa*. Edited by an anonymous "Cateriniano." Roma: E.L.E.V., 1971.

————. *Le Lettere di S. Caterina da Siena, ridotte a miglior lezione, e in ordine nuovo disposte con note di Niccoló Tommaseo a cura di Piero Misciattelli*. Siena: Giuntini e Bentivoglio, 1913–1922.

————. *Epistolario di Santa Caterina da Siena* (Vol. I). Edited by Eugenio Dupré-Theseider. Roma: Istituto Storico per il Medio Evo, 1940.

————. *The Dialogue*. Translated by Suzanne Noffke, O.P. New York: Paulist Press, 1980.

D'Urso, Giacinto. "Il pensiero di S. Caterina e le Sue fonti," *Sapienza* 7 (1954), pp. 335–388.

Fawtier, Robert. *Sainte Catherine de Sienne: Essaie de critique des sources*, Vol. I, *Sources hagiographiques*. Paris: De Boccard, 1921.

————. *Sainte Catherine de Sienne: Essaie de critique des sources*, Vol. II, *Les oeuvres de Sainte Catherine de Sienne*. Paris: De Boccard, 1930.

Gigli, Girolamo. *Vocabolario Cateriniano*. Siena: Vincenzo Pazzini Carli e Figli, 1797.

Grion, Alvaro. *Santa Caterina da Siena: dottrina e fonti*. Brescia: Morcelliana, 1953.

Marracci, Ippolito. *Vindicatio S. Catharinae Senensis a commentitia revelatione ei-dem S. Catharinae Senensi adscripta contra Immaculatam Conceptionem Beatis-simae Virginis Mariae.* Puteoli, 1663.

Processo Castellano, Il. Edited by Marie-Hyacinthe Laurent in *Fontes Vitae S. Catharinae Senensis Historici,* Vol. IX. Milano: Bocca, 1942.

Raymond of Capua. *The Life of Catherine of Siena.* Translated by Conleth Kearns, O.P. Wilmington: Michael Glazier, Inc., 1980.

Taurisano, Innocenzo. *I Fioretti di Santa Caterina da Siena.* Roma: Ferrari, 1927 (2nd edition).

Thomas Antonii de Senis (Caffarini). *Leggenda minore di S. Caterina da Siena e lettere dei suoi discepoli.* Edited by Francesco Grottanelli. Bologna: Romag-noli, 1868.

————. *Libellus de Supplemento Legende prolixe Virginis Beate Catherine de Senis.* Edited by Giuliana Cavallini and Imelda Foralosso. Roma: Edizioni Cather-iniane, 1974.

INDEX TO INTRODUCTIONS AND NOTES

251

INDEX TO TEXT

254

Prayer, 64, 66, 123.
Pride, 72, 217.
Providence, 36, 60, 120.
Prudence, 131, 152, 157.
Purity, 101, 103, 216.

Redemption, 73, 74, 78, 127, 133, 156, 186, 189, 201, 214.

Sacraments, 208.
Schism, 35–36.
Selfishness, 170, 197–198, 208, 217.
Simplicity, 38, 69, 71, 105, 131, 132.
Sin, 25, 71, 72, 73, 74, 89, 93, 99, 104, 105, 112, 113, 119, 172.
Son, God, 16, 102; as wisdom, 16, 35, 42, 43, 48, 78, 105; as Word, 109, 111, 127, 141–142, 171; incarnation, 17, 35, 43, 58, 74, 90, 108–109, 110, 148, 156–165, 202; cf. also Christ.
Soul, powers of, 103, 131, 147, 151, 188.
Strength, 91–92, 143–144.

Suffering, 73, 102, 111, 175, 178, 179, 225.

Tears, 150.
Thanksgiving, 39, 60–61, 64–65, 73, 80, 82.
Thomas, Apostle, 58.
Time, 26, 72, 83, 171, 175.
Trinity, 42, 78, 81, 141, 156, 158–160, 177–178; imaged, 16, 42, 90, 100, 102, 105, 197; cf. also God.
Truth, 70, 78, 79–80, 89, 91, 92, 105, 109, 133, 142, 151, 173, 193–194, 207.

Understanding, 16, 42, 91, 103, 108, 151, 188, 208.

Virtue, 81, 89, 142, 143.

Will, 17, 42, 73, 88, 103, 120–121, 130, 151, 161–162, 188; selfish, 87, 93, 100.
Wisdom, 64, 91, 109.